Foundations

Foundations

Creating Impact in a Globalised World

Luc Tayart de Borms

John Wiley & Sons, Ltd

Other Wiley Editorial Offices

John Wiley & Sons Inc., 111 River Street, Hoboken, NJ 07030, USA

Jossey-Bass, 989 Market Street, San Francisco, CA 94103-1741, USA

Wiley-VCH Verlag GmbH, Boschstr. 12, D-69469 Weinheim, Germany

John Wiley & Sons Australia Ltd, 33 Park Road, Milton, Queensland 4064, Australia

John Wiley & Sons (Asia) Pte Ltd, 2 Clementi Loop #02-01, Jin Xing Distripark, Singapore 129809

John Wiley & Sons Canada Ltd, 22 Worcester Road, Etobicoke, Ontario, Canada M9W 1L1

Wiley also publishes its books in a variety of electronic formats. Some content that appears in
print may not be available in electronic books.

Library of Congress Cataloging in Publication Data

Tayart de Borms, Luc.
   Foundations : creating impact in a globalised world / Luc Tayart de Borms.
     p.   cm.
   Includes index.
   ISBN-13 978-0-470-01505-6
   ISBN-10 0-470-01505-5
   1. Nonprofit organizations.   2. Charitable uses, trusts, and foundations.   I. Title.
   HD62.6.T39 2005
   658′.048—dc22   2005002375

British Library Cataloguing in Publication Data

A catalogue record for this book is available from the British Library

ISBN-13 978-0-470-01505-6 (HB)
ISBN-10 0-470-01505-5 (HB)

Typeset in 11/15pt Goudy by Integra Software Services Pvt. Ltd, Pondicherry, India
Printed and bound in Great Britain by TJ International Ltd, Padstow, Cornwall, UK
This book is printed on acid-free paper responsibly manufactured from sustainable forestry
in which at least two trees are planted for each one used for paper production.

Contents

Foreword

By Stephan Schmidheiny, Founder of the AVINA Foundation

Having founded, funded and – for almost 10 years – presided over a foundation, I feel I have earned the right to be frank about them. I intended to be provocative in writing this foreword. However, on reading Luc Tayart's incisive book on foundations in general, and the future of European foundations in particular, I find I do not have to be critical. He has done the critical thinking and writing for me.

He asks the tough questions: "Give me a good reason why society should support foundations? Do the social benefits outweigh their costs? Are they an effective vehicle for philanthropy? How can such elitist organisations claim to work towards the common, public good?"

It fascinates me that such questions can still be good ones after foundations have been around for so long.

I have heard it cogently argued in the United States that endowed foundations are the only real vehicle for social change because they are not bound by the need to be re-elected, to raise funds, or to make profit. I have heard it equally convincingly argued that foundations retard progress in social development and the arts because their founders, officers and boards are the epitome of the establishment – an establishment that hardly wants to change the very rules that helped them to achieve the exalted position they enjoy.

Try to force knowledgeable Americans to name a concrete accomplishment of any foundation in their country and they usually arrive at two: Carnegie's spreading of public libraries across the country and Rockefeller's eradication of the debilitating screw-worm fly. What would the concrete accomplishments be in Europe?

[An aside: when I question the worth of foundations, I certainly do not mean to question the worth of my own foundation, the AVINA Foundation, which is of course different from all other foundations. We all feel our creations are unique!]

AVINA suffers exactly the same challenges as other foundations: how to be accountable and transparent, how to partner with foundations and all the other organisations that are not foundations, how to measure and evaluate impacts, and – most important – how to move beyond grant-making to become a partner for real social change.

Foundations: Creating Impact in a Globalised World does not answer all of these questions, but it leads readers towards their own answers. It also makes one thing abundantly clear: foundations *must* change. There has been tremendous pressure on corporations to be more transparent, to listen to stakeholders, to learn and be accountable. Companies only control shareholders' money, while most foundations are opaque. They do not listen to stakeholders, nor are they accountable.

Foundations, in the sense that they do not pay taxes, control some of all taxpayers' money. As a result, they are going to be increasingly scrutinised by society and be held more and more accountable. They will have to be at least as responsive as companies. Because they act for the public good, shouldn't they behave better than companies?

They will also have to match themselves against the corporate world in terms of management effectiveness and what can only be called an entrepreneurial spirit. It is hard to do things cost-effectively and with entrepreneurial flair when there is no driving bottom line. We have the good example before us of social entrepreneurs who leverage few resources and much energy into big societal gains. Don't we have a right to expect "socially entrepreneurial foundations" to leverage great resources and energy into big societal gains?

I like the notion in Chapter 8 of foundations working in terms of risk-adjusted returns. Just as fund managers and their clients make a decision to take on increased risk in a search for higher returns, likewise foundation managers should take on increased risk to gain increased returns from the foundation's activities.

Luc Tayart is clear that, "if a foundation is truly to exercise its role of social or political change or as a convenor, it is almost forced into partnerships with other players". Yet it is very hard to have an equal, open, sincere partnership when one partner needs money and the other has it. AVINA has made partnerships with leaders the focal point of its activities; we have found it difficult, but worth trying to get it right.

This is why I am so impressed by Luc Tayart's accomplishment in pioneering the creation of the Network of European Foundations for Innovative Cooperation, which, to be transparent, I also participate in through the Mercator Fund.

Another virtue of the book: it deals with tough questions, but never offers simplistic answers. It is clear on the challenges of moving "beyond grant-making" and on the difficulties of dealing with the many different models of civil society that exist in Europe. It is also willing to be firm amid controversy. It clearly tells European foundations that they should voluntarily move towards a minimum pay-out, or annual amount spent in philanthropy, recommending the 5% figure enshrined in US law.

I wish this book had been available 10 years ago when I founded AVINA; it would have saved us some trial and error. However, I did try to create by instinct and through my own professional background the sort of foundation Luc Tayart calls for: entrepreneurial, business-like (in the best senses), risk-taking and partnering.

In 2003 I handed over the AVINA presidency and created the VIVA Trust, to which I donated the stock in the Latin American holding company I founded, GrupoNueva. It has created an interesting model. The foundation is not a "corporate foundation", but company profits do fund AVINA. This has given company executives a greater interest in the social and environmental realities of Latin America, where AVINA operates. The link has driven AVINA leadership to want to make it more efficient and well managed.

Today, AVINA is trying to encourage leaders to form networks for change and encouraging links among leaders of business and civil society. It is becoming more of a service organisation than a funding one and is borrowing the best management techniques from the best in the business. But it still has a lot to learn, so I'll be sending many copies of this book to my friends at AVINA!

I want to end by thanking Luc Tayart for his efforts both in producing this fine study and for yet another of his attempts to open the minds and horizons of those managing big foundations.

Introduction

The objective of this book is to spark a discussion both inside and outside the sector about the *raison d'être* of foundations. After 20 years of being a practitioner in the sector, I felt compelled to "go public" with some of the concerns and aspirations I have. This book is written from a European perspective, which explains its style. It is more critical and dialectical compared to the American approach, which tends to see the good and the positive in the sector first and foremost.

I hope I am not accused of trying to "preach the truth" because the ideas presented here are indeed a work in progress. I am trying to deliver clear messages, but I do so in modesty, for these are the views of a single practitioner, not an academic. In modesty also because in the face of so much diversity in the sector, it is dangerous to draw generalisations.

There has not been much reflection inside the sector, despite recent scrutiny from the media, politicians and the public. For the most part, we work inside our associations and clubs, occasionally exploring such existential questions from an academic perspective. When confronted with a scandal, we tend to circle the wagons and retreat amidst a cloud of self-justification. Foundations are deeply embedded in the establishment, even though we are often regarded as the voice of civil society. As a result, we enjoy considerable status.

Over the years, I have begun to believe that foundation leaders and practitioners have been seduced by our idealism. We have slipped into moral certainty – a very seductive and potentially very self-destructive emotional state when we are confronted with political realities.

The truth is that foundations are caught in an accountability squeeze. And rightly so. We are, for the most part, unaccountable organisations that enjoy considerable freedom at the expense of taxpayer contributions. Collectively, we have the ability to mobilise an important amount of financial and human resources. There is an ocean of rich knowledge and valuable experience locked up inside the sector.

Because of our position of exceptional privilege, I believe we must critically examine our roles with a view to fulfilling our obligation to create value. At the same time, we must take value creation to a different level. Some believe that our work might be better and more efficiently accomplished by other non-profit organisations or even governments. In some instances, they have been proved right.

I make a plea for foundations to prove their social legitimacy by thinking about their work more strategically, as a continuum that embraces many roles, but is focused on value creation, the achievement of specific objectives and meaningful impact assessment. I also make a plea for foundations to reach beyond traditional grant-making activity and become active, engaged, value-added members of civil society. Foundations need to take on different roles, while deploying a careful mix of several methodologies.

Stakeholders as well as the wider community must become engaged because foundations are not endowed with democratic legitimacy. It is time for foundations to move beyond alleviating social and political problems by making modest – often unquantifiable – "improvements" to society, as valuable as this work is, and will continue to be. But we must act more strategically.

A future role that I believe is critical is one of "convenor", for lack of a better word. In this way foundations can play a critical role by presenting a platform for informed debate and discussion, to lay the groundwork for informed policy and decision-making that is more inclusive.

In western societies, foundations have the opportunity to develop a more creative approach to complex issues on a local and global level.

This is the next, natural step in the evolution of the role of foundations. It is a function that should be expanded upon and developed as a separate role. This could go a long way to increasing our social legitimacy.

The "impact driven foundation" must move off its traditional neutral territory into a space where it can engage in a frank dialogue with stakeholders, asking tough questions and challenging the status quo. This is not an easy task. This type of engagement is out of character for many and can be risky when dealing with controversial issues. But I believe foundation leaders must take such risks, or risk coming under fire ourselves; or worse, becoming irrelevant.

This book also hopes to be, respectfully, a wake-up call to philanthropists on both sides of the Atlantic. We have faced huge challenges in the past and are continuing to do so as we support countries in Europe and around the world to strengthen civil societies and lay a foundation for democracy. We are fighting racism, poverty, marginalisation and disease.

Today, our task is also to show leadership on global issues because the challenges our societies are facing have global dimensions and require global solutions. Our problems are interconnected. We need to take what works in our initiatives, projects and programmes and take it to the world. We need to turn our vision and our mission statements into reality if we are really to make a difference. At the same time as I am calling on the sector to be more ambitious, I am calling on it to do so with modesty, for we are but one player in society. Therein lies one of many paradoxes.

It is our duty and our responsibility to take what we have learned and contribute to a global architecture that is more inclusive and more just. Many foundations are already doing this. It is my hope that this becomes the rule, rather than the exception.

I hope that this book sparks some much needed soul searching and also gives some practitioners a few ideas about how to achieve more impact. It is not meant as a critique of the good work being done by my colleagues all over the world as they strive to make our world a better place. Rather, it is a call to build on the good work done and take it to another, perhaps more effective, level.

It is impossible to make a list of all of the people who have supported me – directly and indirectly – in this endeavour; the risk of leaving someone out is high. However, I have to thank some directly, beginning with my colleagues and former colleagues at the King Baudouin Foundation (KBF). I am "old furniture" at KBF. Over the 20 years I have spent there, many have contributed to the content of this book, and I must thank them for their engagement and exceptional motivation that has made success stories of many of our projects. Thanks also to the Board of Governors for the trust they have placed in me.

I want to make an exception and mention Michel Didisheim, former CEO and chair of KBF. He not only laid the groundwork for what KBF is today, but also gave me opportunities to test out new ground and discover for myself the boundaries that bind the sector. For this, I cannot thank him enough.

My peers have been a source of inspiration. Through the European Foundation Centre (EFC), the Network of European Foundations for Innovative Cooperation, the Hague Club and the US Council on Foundations (to name but a few), I have come to know very special colleagues with great and challenging ideas. I owe a lot to them. Some of the seeds for this book were sown when, as chair of the EFC, I had the opportunity to put pen to paper for several speeches.

But it was Norine MacDonald, Managing Director of the Gabriel Foundation and The Mercator Fund who, after some weeks of difficult persuasion, convinced me to take on this task. Now that it is accomplished, I am very grateful for her perseverance and insistence, both as a colleague and a friend. I have never harboured an ambition to become an author, but The Mercator Fund and its funder, Stephan Schmidheiny, have made this possible. I particularly want to thank Stephan Schmidheiny, who penned the foreword, for his innovative, global thinking. We can only hope for more such leaders to stand up in our sector.

Running the KBF and writing this book meant a lot of evening and weekend work, but I did not stand alone in this task. Without Dianna Rienstra as my editor, it would never have happened. As a non-mother tongue English speaker, it would have been impossible for me to write this book. It was not just the language issue, but also the cultural concepts behind the language. I believe she has met this challenge in a thoughtful and creative way. It was difficult to go beyond the often-imperfect English phrases I put on paper to get inside my head and grasp my ideas. Again, it is very difficult to put my gratitude into words.

Writing a book was a new adventure; I have always preferred action over talking and surely over writing. But it was a fine experience. Most importantly, however, I hope this book will contribute to shaking up the foundation world somewhat, for the sector holds huge potential.

I apologise for the many references to KBF projects. There are, of course, thousands of very worthy projects out there, but I felt compelled to write about what I know and can only hope the examples are of some interest to practitioners and non-practitioners. Finally, the views expressed here are my own and not those of the King Baudouin Foundation, of which I am currently the Managing Director.

1

Why foundations?

An issue rarely brought into the political arena is that of the *raison d'être* of the foundation[1] in today's modern societies. This is probably fortuitous, considering that there is not a strong theoretical underpinning to why foundations should exist or continue to do so. There has been some soul searching inside the sector, such as those attempting to answer such existential questions in an academic framework or those pushing for a deeper analysis of the outcome of the work of foundations.

Alternatively, there are the justifications posited and the good works lauded in the wake of a scandal, where some, including the media, question their value, stating bluntly: "Give me a good reason why society should support foundations." Other questions arise: "Do the social benefits outweigh their costs? Are they an effective vehicle for philanthropy? How can such elitist organisations claim to work towards the common, public good?" They are, after all, part of the establishment, deeply imbedded in a nation's social structure. They are backed by wealthy donors, often with a powerful network that spans across different segments of society and reaches into the most prestigious boardrooms and backrooms, giving foundations considerable social cachet and political clout.

Foundations are, for the most part, highly unaccountable organisations that enjoy considerable freedom at the expense of valuable taxpayer

---

[1] For the purpose of this book, foundations share three fundamental characteristics: they are independent, they have an endowment, and they operate with a view towards serving the public benefit.

contributions. They use private money for a perceived public benefit that critics claim is rarely if ever measured, evaluated or democratically controlled. Yet supporters of foundations claim they are agents of change, the voice of civil society, innovators, a lynchpin of democratic societies, and much, much more. Theorists paint the roles of foundations in black and white, but in reality, their work is carried out in grey zones that encompass a plethora of roles. Today, a new and dynamic philanthropy is emerging as foundations take on new roles in communities, usually involving several of the dimensions discussed in this chapter.

In our increasingly complex society, the pace of change is accelerating in the wake of liberalisation of markets and privatisation. This paradigm is propelled by globalisation, seen by some as the enemy of change and by others as the only way forward. One thing is certain – globalisation is here to stay. One of the challenges of the twenty-first century is how to make it work for everyone; how best to balance competitiveness with social equity and sustainability, defined by the triple bottom line.[2] In many nations, free trade and the opening of markets is not benefiting society as a whole. Poverty and disease continue to engulf nations, as whole groups of citizens are being marginalised.

Their voices can be heard in multi-stakeholder forums and conferences around the world. Their concerns have been enshrined in the United Nation's Millennium Goals for Development and the ambitious blueprint conceived at the International Conference on Population and Development in 1994. But what is changing? Who is listening? Critics view globalisation as the continuous hegemony of rich nations imposed upon poorer ones. (Witness the breakdown of the WTO Ministerial talks in Cancun, September 2003.)

This has created a climate of mistrust and fear of business, government and international financial institutions, which is widening the gap, making a mutually beneficial dialogue unwieldy if not impossible. At the same time, it has presented foundations with an invaluable

---

[2] The triple bottom line agenda refers to decision- and policy-making with a view to economic prosperity, social justice and environmental quality.

window of opportunity to take on another role, that of convenor. This is not a new concept as foundations have "convened" many meetings, but depending on the level of sophistication of societies in which foundations are working, it has the potential to foster multi-stakeholder dialogue and mutual understanding, which, in turn, can lead to consensus-building and informed policy and decision-making. By also promoting citizen engagement, foundations can become centres of excellence in civil society.

It is a compelling answer to those who are, rightly, questioning the social legitimacy of foundations in western societies.

The impact of the "philanthropic impulse"

All foundations have views on the issues they intend to tackle and the methodologies to accomplish their goals. Behind these views are clear choices, based on assumptions and philosophies of those who created, funded or continue to fund their work. These assumptions and choices fuel the motivation that, in part, drives the "philanthropic impulse", which has a strong impact on the way foundations work.

The interplay between this impulse and the sophistication of the society in which the foundation operates also helps to determine its role in that society. It clearly makes a difference whether the foundation's creator is a venture capitalist, a multinational corporation, or if it was established by a private bequest, the privatisation of a local savings bank, a commemoration of a special occasion (such as an anniversary), or by philanthropically minded royalty.

Although this impulse may evolve over the years, it has a very strong influence over a foundation's behaviour, which should be taken into consideration when judging its issues and methodologies. They all try "to do good", but the strategies they use to achieve this goal differ depending on how they were created and by whom.

However, this reality should not prevent anyone from taking a critical view of foundations and their role in the twenty-first century. This book intends to do precisely that, but taking into consideration this very important dimension.

An obligation to create value

> *Some of the money that foundations give away belongs, in a sense, to all of us. That is why we look to foundations to create real value for society.*
>   Michael Porter and Mark Kramer[3]

If foundations are to thrive and maintain legitimacy in our rapidly globalising world, they must take value creation to a different level in the societies in which they operate. Because of their cost, society expects them to be more than mere conduits for giving. Value creation can be accomplished in many ways, depending on the context and the challenges at hand.

Curiously, until quite recently, there has been little public interest in foundations in the US and almost none in Europe. They have been regarded as a "political detail" that comes to the fore only when under fire. Today, there is no doubt that foundations are coming under closer scrutiny. The high profile work of the Bill and Melinda Gates Foundation, for example, with its annual budget of some $24 billion* and its slogan, "Bringing innovations in health and learning to the global community", are examples that have focused public attention on philanthropy and charity – and their corresponding costs to society in forgone tax revenue.

---

[3] Michael Porter and Mark Kramer, "Philanthropy's new agenda: creating value", *Harvard Business Review*, November–December 1999, p. 122.
* Dollar quantities relate to the US dollar unless otherwise stated.

The Bill and Melinda Gates Foundation spends about $800 million a year on global health, nearly the same as the World Health Organization's annual budget and about as much as the US Agency for International Development gave in 1993 to fight AIDS and other diseases in developing countries.[4] Consider that the United States' contribution to the World Health Organisation totalled $93.6 million in 2003.[5]

Some economists argue that tax revenue forgone translates into government expenditure. In this context, one might query whether the work of foundations might be better and more efficiently accomplished by non-profit organisations or even by governments.

Do the math

Does the public know that when a foundation receives a donation, most of the gift sits on the sidelines? Foundations do not invest all of their assets to philanthropic causes. In fact, Michael Porter and Mark Kramer report that, in the US, just 0.01% of foundation investment portfolios is invested to support philanthropic purposes.

Foundations are also busy creating financial returns because they have an obligation to its donors and trustees to invest its assets. This is a function of their perpetuity.

On average, they note, US foundations donate just 5.5% of their assets to charity each year, a number slightly above the US legal minimum of 5%. Helmut Anheier and Diana Leat maintain that, in Britain, very few foundations meet the 5% payout rate, which is not mandatory.[6] A 2003 survey by the European Foundation Centre

---

[4] Tom Paulson, "Gates Foundation out to break the cycle of disease", *Seattle Post Intelligencer*, 8 December 2003.

[5] http://whqmarcopolo.who.int/rbcont/RBRetrieve.asp

[6] Helmut Anheier and Diana Leat, "From charity to creativity: philanthropic foundations in the 21st century", *Comedia*, 2002, p. 69.

of 13 foundations, revealed an average spending (payout) rate of 3.34%.

This example serves to illustrate the point. Across Europe, the numbers may differ depending on the national tax treatment of giving. Nonetheless, in general, the difference between direct giving to NGOs and giving through foundations is enormous. When an individual contributes €100 to a charitable organisation, the nation loses €40 in tax revenue, but the charity gains €100, which is used to provide services to society. The immediate social benefit, then, is 250% of the lost tax revenue. When €100 is contributed to a foundation, the nation loses the same €40, but the immediate social benefit is just the €5.50 per year that the foundation gives away – that is, less than 14% of the forgone tax revenue.

At the same time, it must be remembered that this reasoning stems from a short-term view, for example, when reviewing an annual budget. Foundations have always argued that they take a longer-term view for a number of reasons, such as their need to address the issues of perpetuity and to create intergenerational equity. (This is discussed further in Chapter 5.)

Given that foundations in many countries pay almost no tax on the appreciation of assets, the forgone tax revenue grows even larger. When the stock market was in its boom phase in the 1990s, the US government lost tax revenue of $0.75 for every dollar the foundations gave to social enterprises. In effect, the US, as a nation, is paying up front for deferred social benefits.[7]

Considering the administrative costs of both foundations and grantees that must comply with unwieldy application and qualification requirements, this could be considered a rather expensive way to allocate money to social enterprises.

---

[7] Michael Porter and Mark Kramer, "Philanthropy's new agenda: creating value", *Harvard Business Review*, November–December 1999, p. 122.

A question of accountability

In this light, it can be argued that foundations have an even greater need to be accountable not only to their donor(s) and grantees, but to society as a whole. US foundations are increasingly under pressure to evaluate their work and increase transparency, particularly in the light of scandals in the past few years over such issues as CEO's and board members' remuneration and perks. They must not only create value, they must also be seen to do so to justify their exceptional privileges, particularly their exemption from taxation.

Michael Porter and Mark Kramer challenge foundations to create value and point out the following:

> Improving the performance of philanthropy would enable foundations to have a much greater impact on society. Foundations could play a leading role in changing the culture of social sector management. They could spearhead the evolution of philanthropy from private acts of conscience into a professional field. Until foundations accept their accountability to society and meet their obligation to create value, they exist in a world where they cannot fail. Unfortunately, they also cannot truly succeed.[8]

This is a challenge to foundations everywhere, as they grapple to prove their social legitimacy to a wide range of players, including their peers. Evaluation is an essential element in this process, which means that foundations must be courageous enough to recognise and learn from failures.

It is critical that foundations start thinking about their work strategically, as a continuum that embraces many roles, but is focused on value creation, the achievement of specific objectives and meaningful impact assessment. This should be the new ethical imperative of the foundation in the twenty-first century.

---

[8] Michael Porter and Mark Kramer, "Philanthropy's new agenda: creating value", *Harvard Business Review*, November–December 1999, p. 130.

Added value

Added value is a commonly used concept, prevalent in corporate and management literature. Recently, it has become a buzzword or a leitmotif in literature concerning the philanthropic sector. The concept of added value changes in various contexts, but what does it mean for the work of foundations?

In economic literature, it is frequently referred to as the process of changing or transforming a product from its original state into a more valuable state that is more attractive to the market. More interesting, in relation to this chapter, is the question of how added value can be achieved. Management literature states that it can be achieved through innovation and/or coordination. Innovation refers to improving existing processes, procedures, products and services or creating new ones, and coordination can be horizontal or vertical. Horizontal coordination entails pooling or consolidating from the same level of the production or service chain; vertical coordination involves agreements and dialogues across the various levels of production and service delivery.

These two forms of creating added value approach the concepts discussed in this chapter, specifically regarding the role of foundations to create added value through their work as catalysts of social and political change (innovation) or their role as convenors (coordination).

The role of foundations

Foundations perform a myriad of roles in today's society, many simultaneously and many overlapping (Figure 1.1). In addition, foundations often find themselves fulfilling numerous roles through their support to diverse groups in society. These roles are different, depending on the societies in which they are working. To better understand these roles, it is useful to start with a general definition, or description. The

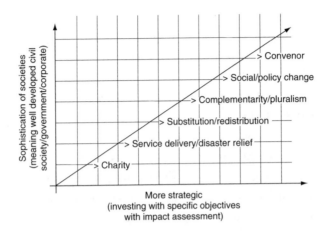

Figure 1.1 Spectrum of foundation practice

European Foundation Centre (EFC) describes foundations as a diverse community with a common aim of associating private wealth to benefit the public. EFC maintains:

> The role and activities of foundations are driven by a public benefit purpose and a general philanthropic impulse which aims at an improvement in the living conditions and quality of life of the general public and specific disadvantaged groups and individuals, as well as promoting civic initiatives and active citizenship.[9]

This is quite a broad mandate. In exercising it, foundations cover an equally broad spectrum of roles and perform many functions, described in the literature as ranging from charity, disaster relief, service delivery, substitution, redistribution, pluralism and complementarity, to that of a catalyst of policy and social change. Foundations enjoy a unique position in society, as they are independent from market considerations and politics. As a result, they are able to operate in a neutral middle ground, outside the commercial sector and the state.

In practice, foundations play more than one role or several roles concurrently, depending on the nature of their work and the level of sophistication of the societies in which they operate. All are equally

---

[9]European Foundation Centre, *Working with Foundations in Europe: Why and How?* January 2001, p. 1. http://www.efc.be

important. The exact role or roles are defined more by time and place. For example, disaster relief, which can take the form of service delivery, is critical in some countries in Africa as entire generations are being devastated by the HIV/AIDS pandemic. In many areas, there is no civil society. A foundation supporting an HIV/AIDS prevention programme or the creation of clinics, for example, is playing the roles of disaster relief, service delivery, and perhaps substitution for action by the state.

Increasingly, in relatively developed societies, foundations play the role of catalyst of policy and social change. For example, the EFC views the role of some European foundations over the last decade as one of advancing cooperation by supporting the development of fledgling democracies and emerging market economies in central and eastern Europe. Foundations support the creation of the Single Market by operating across borders and developing cooperation schemes at European level. In this way, they promote European solidarity and integration.

This type of strategic philanthropy is based on trying to tackle the root causes of societal "problems" rather than applying quick-fix band-aid solutions. It is a model based on the concept of empowerment, which is much more than a buzzword in the development community today; it is a tenet that is redirecting policy and actions by governments, NGOs, international institutions and civil society.

A new role is emerging for foundations – a role that several foundations are already assuming. This new role involves moving from the reactive into the realm of the proactive to become "convenors", by providing a neutral platform for discussion, informed debate and consensus-building around highly charged issues. Acting as a convenor, a foundation can create a space that brings all stakeholders together in a forum where no stakeholder dominates the agenda and where constructive mutual engagement has a chance to result in mutually beneficial outcomes.

Charity: an institution or organisation helping those in need

In the early twentieth century the work of many American and some European foundations shifted from charity to philanthropy – that is, from an institution or organisation for helping those in need (typically through a one-off gift or donation) to one that is aimed at changing the deeper conditions that caused the problem in the first place.

The distinction between the two is obvious, but they share the common element of relieving human suffering – poverty alleviation, hunger, and health care, for example – through private investment in an often loosely defined common good.

The EFC notes that today's foundations place a greater emphasis on empowering individuals and increasing citizen participation by strengthening civil society. The foundation landscape in Europe is "richly varied", with some 200000 engaged in a wide variety of programming activities.

Author and professor Helmut Anheier notes that in Europe, foundations either operate or pursue their objectives by a combination of grant-making activities with the running of their own institutions, programmes and projects. Historically, they were operating institutions such as schools, orphanages or hospitals, although many distributed money and contributions in kind.

The sharp distinction between grant-making and operating foundations, which is not as relevant today, emerged much later historically and for the US and Europe is a phenomenon of both the nineteenth and early twentieth centuries.[10]

Disaster relief and service delivery

The roles of supporting disaster relief and service delivery are very often overlapping as humanitarian interventions increasingly include a development dimension. In filling the gap between the two, often referred to as "the grey zone", disaster relief and service delivery activities often blur. Disaster relief speaks for itself and does not need an explanation. However, populations are more vulnerable to natural or

---

[10] Helmut Anheier, *Foundations in Europe: A Comparative Perspective*, Civil Society Working Paper 18, August 2001, p. 4.

man-made disaster (such as conflict) and thus require increased service delivery in societies where the social fabric has been severely torn by poverty, disease, lack of education, and the absence of good governance by public authorities.

Often there is no infrastructure by which to deliver relief, or a state with the authority and means of taking care of its citizens. An obvious example is the HIV/AIDS pandemic in several war-torn African nations and the unfolding human crises caused by malaria and tuberculosis, which also require disaster relief and service delivery, or a hybrid of the two.

Institutional donors such as the EU are responding to these global challenges through development programmes that focus on poverty reduction, empowerment and support for infrastructure. Private donors, such as foundations, provide grants to civil society and other grantees to support NGOs and the civil society organisations on the ground that deliver the assistance.

This is an obvious example of how time, place and the level of sophistication of a society are critical factors in defining a foundation's role. It is also important to consider the danger unfolding in the wake of the trend towards strategic philanthropy in that foundations may lose sight of the invaluable role they play in supporting disaster relief and service delivery in developing countries.

Service delivery is a popular foundation activity expressed through building schools, institutes for those with special needs, hospitals, hospices, shelters for women or the homeless, food banks, and so on. The degree of service delivery is usually determined by the nature of civil society and the role of the state in the particular country.

Theotokos Foundation

Service delivery and much more

Since 1963, the Theotokos Foundation, Ilion Greece, a private, non-profit organisation, has offered comprehensive services to children and youths up to 25 years of age with learning and other developmental disabilities. However, the foundation plays several roles. For example, Theotokos is also certified as a training centre for Continuing Adult training, offering yearly courses on rehabilitation and educational intervention for clients with learning disabilities. The courses are targeted at the unemployed or employees of the current welfare system. The foundation also participates in several EU-funded programmes, such as the European Social Fund.[11]

Redistribution and substitution

Several authors describe the role of foundations as one of redistribution in that their added value takes the form of a voluntary redistribution of wealth. Helmut Anheier and Diana Leat postulate that many foundations target funding work in particularly disadvantaged communities, hoping in some way to correct a societal imbalance and equalise the distribution of resources.

> Redistribution of resources is obviously an attractive goal . . . It helps to create a fairer society without radical, social and economic upheaval. Another is that it is essential to the longer-term sustainability of existing social and economic arrangements. In other words, redistribution is a way of dealing with the damaging side effects of a market system.[12]

Kenneth Prewitt points out that charitable giving in general, and foundation grant-making in particular, is considered to be redistributive, and that is assumed to be so because of the tax benefit involved, particularly in the US. Wealth that establishes foundations comes from the richest strata of society, and because they sponsor programmes that disproportionately benefit the lower income strata, it can be claimed that redistribution occurs. He questions whether foundation funds are

---

[11] http://www.theotokos.gr
[12] Helmut Anheier and Diana Leat, "From charity to creativity: philanthropic foundations in the 21st century", *Comedia*, 2002, p. 80.

more redistributive than if they had been taxed in the first place, but maintains that they can potentially fulfil this role.[13]

In Europe, individuals face much higher taxation rates, which results in a much different reality. Generally, the solidarity theoretically created by redistribution is delivered through the tax system with the objective of creating greater social cohesion.

The role of foundations can also be one of substitution, when a state or market fails to deliver services to its citizens, or the service sector is stretched beyond its limit. In this role, the foundation "substitutes" state action in the public sector by filling in the gaps created by this shortfall.

The Grocers' Charity

Redistributing resources and filling in the gaps

The Grocers' Charity, the charitable brand of The Worshipful Company of Grocers and a Livery Company of the City of London, distributes funds primarily in the field of education, but also in poverty relief, medicine, disability, churches, heritage, the arts and the elderly. For example, its poverty relief initiatives provide funding to projects that focus on children and young people, particularly those at risk, to build confidence, share skills and create opportunity.

The major proportion of funding in education is donated to establishments with links to the Grocers' Company for internal scholarships and bursaries. It makes donations to a variety of organisations that provide support and services to people with disabilities of all ages and supports causes that improve medical facilities for the ill, including

---

[13] Kenneth Prewitt, "The importance of foundations in an open society", *The Future of Foundations in an Open Society*, Bertelsmann Foundation Publishers, 1999, pp. 20–21.

research. The Grocers' Charity also supports facilities and initiatives that benefit the frail elderly and provide them with care services to enable them to stay in their homes.

(Today, charitable fund-raising for the benefit of education, housing and church bodies has for the most part replaced many of the original trade functions of the Livery Companies.[14])

Fostering pluralism and complementarity

Pluralism is one of the hallmarks of a democratic and open society, typically expressed by civil society, NGOs, trades unions and other associations. It is also expressed outside of mainstream politics through the voices of minorities, socially excluded groups or the disadvantaged (including those with disabilities) who have difficulty being heard by or gaining access to political institutions.

Anheier and Leat argue: "The very fact that foundations can operate outside the political system of parties, government and public administration creates opportunities for support of causes that are either bypassed or unwelcome to mainstream politics."[15] As such, they maintain, foundations can provide support and compensate for democratic deficits.

Others claim that foundations act as the voice of civil society, or its "development arm", as they build social capital. The EFC views foundations as an expression of civic awareness of responsibility towards the community and, as a result, represent "an indispensable element of an active civil society expressly protected by the rule of law".[16]

[14] http://www.grocershall.co.uk/
[15] Helmut Anheier and Diana Leat, "From charity to creativity: philanthropic foundations in the 21st century", Comedia, 2002, p. 74.
[16] European Foundation Centre, Working with Foundations in Europe: Why and How? January 2001, p. 2. http://www.efc.be

Prewitt maintains that foundation funds within the non-profit sector can promote "ideological diversity and service differentiation". Foundations play a critical role in funding the "unusual or the unexpected because they are not beholden to the consensus-forcing demands placed on the public sector". Foundations intensify the natural diversity of the non-profit sector, thereby contributing to pluralism. He continues:

> If foundations can help create and preserve pluralism, can help in the search for common human values without losing sight of the diversity of belief and practice, they will have earned a legitimate place in our open society.[17]

This type of activity often casts foundations in the role of fostering complementarity in that they support and fund what governments do not. Promoting innovation is a role closely associated with these activities, and one that, most agree, foundations perform very well.

Evrika Foundation

Encouraging excellence through complimentarity

The Evrika Foundation, Sofia, promotes projects involving talented Bulgarian children and young people in the areas of science, technology and entrepreneurship, as well as fostering international cooperation in these areas. In addition, it supports young inventors, scientists and entrepreneurs and participates in the dissemination of scientific, technological and economic knowledge.

Evrika organises and participates in the organisation and financing of special national schools and summer universities in science, technical

---

[17] Kenneth Prewitt, "The importance of foundations in an open society", *The Future of Foundations in an Open Society*, Bertelsmann Foundation Publishers, 1999, p. 9.

studies, technologies, and management. It also assists young researchers and experts up to the age of 35 by covering part of the expenses for participating in international congresses, symposia, and conferences.[18]

The Joseph Rowntree Charitable Trust (JRCT)

Racial Justice Programme fosters pluralism

One of Britain's larger trusts, the York-based JRCT, makes about 170 to 200 grants annually, totalling some £4 million. It seeks to promote racial justice and equal opportunity as a basis for a harmonious, multi-racial, multi-ethnic society in the UK. Outside Britain it makes grants for work towards peace, justice and reconciliation in South Africa and in Ireland. The JRCT promotes problem-solving through innovative, radical solutions that make a difference.

Its Racial Justice Programme works at local, national and European level. The aim of the West Yorkshire Programme, launched in 1992, was to promote the full participation of racially disadvantaged groups in community life. It supports projects working for equality, social justice and civil rights in the Authorities of Bradford, Calderdale, Kirklees, Leeds and Wakefield.

This complements JRCT's work at national level to support projects that promote issues of racial justice with policy-shapers, decision-makers and opinion-formers and encouraging black and ethnic minority people-led organisations to contribute to policy development and participate at planning and decision-making levels.

---

[18] http://www.evrika.org

At European level, JRCT supports projects working to promote awareness among policy-makers and within the European institutions of the need to protect the human rights of minority communities, asylum-seekers and migrants as well as those working for a more accountable and open process for developing EU policy in relation to race and immigration.[19]

A catalyst of social and political change

Critics claim that foundations are not and cannot be agents of social and political change and that even to postulate this notion is a form self-aggrandisement. Others, such as Anheier and Leat, call for a greater research effort to examine this issue more closely, yet acknowledge that some see it as a more focused and realistic role for foundations.[20] Several case studies, however, reveal that foundations can effect social and political change. For example, foundations played a role, albeit a small one, in the US civil rights movement and in defeating apartheid in South Africa. In Europe, for example, foundations have helped to create or even re-create civil society, as well as fund research institutes. This was a particularly strong trend in the former Central and Eastern European countries.

It is argued that a foundation operates on the basis of strategic choices about what can lead to a desired social change. Prewitt points to the core principle that new knowledge and new technologies, and more equitable application of knowledge, is a powerful engine of social

---

[19] http://www.jrct.org.uk
[20] Helmut Anheier and Diana Leat, "From charity to creativity: philanthropic foundations in the 21st century", Comedia, 2002, p. 87.

improvement. The Rockefeller Foundation abided by this strategy with its heavy investment in medical and public health research and, later, in agronomic research that helped to galvanise the green revolution.[21]

EFC views foundations as often playing a valuable role as leaders, daring to venture forth into contentious territory, where government dares not. Foundations help to bring about far-reaching change, including the search for innovative solutions to problems through promoting academic, scientific and new technology programmes, and they introduce new variables into society's discourse. EFC maintains that foundations are one of the driving forces behind social change as well as being benefactor institutions for the public at large.[22]

Today, trying to bring about social and political change is a fundamental principle of those founding, funding and working in foundations. They view foundations as critical catalysts. Porter and Kramer state that foundations "can and should" lead social progress:

> They have the potential to make more effective use of scarce resources than either individual donors or the government. Free from political pressures, foundations can explore new solutions to social problems with an independence that government can never have.[23]

Foundations, they argue, have the scale, the time horizon, and the professional management to create benefits for society more effectively. Whether they live up to this potential is another matter altogether.

---

[21] Kenneth Prewitt, "The importance of foundations in an open society", *The Future of Foundations in an Open Society*, Bertelsmann Foundation Publishers, 1999, p. 6.

[22] European Foundation Centre, *Working with Foundations in Europe: Why and How?* January 2001, p. 2. http://www.efc.be

[23] Michael Porter and Mark Kramer, "Philanthropy's new agenda: creating value", *Harvard Business Review*, November–December 1999, p. 122.

Jaume Bofill Foundation

Fostering a better understanding of society

The Jaume Bofill Foundation, located in Barcelona, aims to undertake critical analyses of society, its structural bases, mechanisms of operation and processes of integration and marginalisation to which they give rise. Its projects challenge the established order and study and combat all forms of inequality. These aims contribute to asserting Catalonia's national identity within the framework of the respect and promotion of people's rights.

Four years ago, foundation trustees established priority areas of action targeted at achieving the overall aim of the betterment of Catalan society: reinforcement of democratic society, attention to immigrants, improvements in education, and cultural development.

For example, the foundation supported the development of Citizens' Councils and the launch of Democracía.web under an agreement with the Catalan parliament, which aimed to bring its activities closer to the citizens through the use of new technologies. Grants are given to associations run by immigrants themselves or to organisations assisting these groups. The foundation promotes education through its Senderi programme and funded an analysis of the impact of the new information and communication technologies in Catalan society.

Although the foundation declares itself to be independent, it says that this does not amount to neutrality towards the major ideological, political, social and moral issues facing Catalan society and the world.[24]

---

[24] http://www.fbofill.org

The way forward: the foundation as convenor

A concept that has found its way into the lexicon of the twenty-first century is "sustainability", whereby government, companies, civil society and others are measured against the triple bottom line. Sustainability, the principle of ensuring that our actions today do not limit the range of economic, social and environmental options open to future generations, is the backbone of the emerging development paradigm. The triple bottom line agenda is fast evolving on a broad front, with one of the most challenging tasks being that of coordinated delivery to ensure both efficiency and effectiveness in resource use.

However, sustainability means different things to many people. The language of government and business is changing: multi-stakeholder dialogue, social inclusion, consultation, social linkages, capacity-building, empowerment, to name a few. Many of these "multi-stakeholders" view consultation as a smoke screen, or an attempt to "greenwash" pre-existing agendas such as protectionism and the promotion of unfettered capitalism. Such views are symptomatic of a breakdown of trust.

A sobering wake up call: the breakdown of trust

The World Economic Forum's 2002 Voice of the People survey of 36 000 citizens across 47 countries on six continents showed that people around the world express the lowest levels of trust in national legislative bodies and large, global companies. The highest levels of trust world wide are enjoyed by the armed forces, NGOs and the United Nations. (Respondents were asked to rate their level of trust in 17 different institutions to operate in the best interest of society. Results of the survey sample are statistically representative of the views of 1.4 billion citizens.)

Around the world, the principal democratic institution in each country (parliament, congress) is the least trusted of the 17 institutions tested. Two-thirds of those surveyed do not agree that their country is "governed by the will of the people", and citizens have as much trust in the media and in trades unions as they have in their national (mostly elected) governments.[25]

It is unlikely that citizens around the world have increased their level of trust since the 2002 survey.

Multi-stakeholders need a neutral forum

In today's climate of mistrust and fear, governments and politicians are often viewed as prisoners of the electorate and the muscle of big business. Civil society and other organisations have their own agendas, determined by the political realities presented by the expectations of their members or donors. International organisations do not have the public space or institutional structures to listen to individual voices.

Foundations can – and should – play a critical role in helping to resolve this conundrum by presenting a neutral platform for informed debate and discussion, to lay the groundwork for informed policy and decision-making that is more inclusive. The EFC defines an important role for foundations in bringing new players to the decision-making table, thereby developing a more community-based process of change-making. This trend is increasing with foundations being set up to help local communities to address social, economic and environmental challenges.[26] In addition, foundations are increasingly being called upon to support civil society and other organisations to address global issues.

To a certain extent, foundations already play this role, which fits in with their obligation to promote innovation, both in ideas and in practice, and as a catalyst for change. As convenor, foundations do not

---

[25] http://www.weforum.org/site/homepublic.nsf/Content/Annual+Meeting+2003

[26] European Foundation Centre, *Working with Foundations in Europe: Why and How?* January 2001, p. 2. http://www.efc.be

operate on their own social or political change agenda, but they rather embrace a broad spectrum of roles, driven by the notion of engagement in an atmosphere of mutual learning and mutual respect. Foundations that act within the framework of highly complex, developed societies can create a unique value added, through developing a more creative approach to complex issues on a local and global level.

This is the next, natural step in the evolution of the role of foundations. It is a function that should be expanded and developed as a separate role. It could go a long way towards increasing their social legitimacy.

King Baudouin Foundation

Coming to terms with food safety

Belgium has lurched from one food crisis to another over the past 10 years, leaving in their wake wary consumers, an embattled industry, confused public authorities and defeatist farmers. Companies and educational establishments active in animal production decided not to sit on the sidelines but to overcome their frustration and open a social dialogue involving all stakeholders and interest groups, such as the government, animal welfare organisations, consumer groups, and the distribution sector.

Organisations representing the various stakeholders came together to form the non-profit association Animal Production in the 21st Century (Dierlijke Productie in de 21ste eeuw, DP21 vzw). Recognising the need for a neutral forum, DP21 vzw approached the Brussels-based King Baudouin Foundation, which brought in the regional Flanders government. The Animal Production & Consumption in the 21st Century project was launched, with the objective of arriving at shared views with all the stakeholders in Flanders. It also aimed to identify society's needs in this area as well as the basic requirements for animal production and consumption.

Working together with Global Business Network Europe, which specialises in developing strategic policy processes, participants developed three scenarios, which they used to map images of the future. Rather than having a predictive role, they anticipated possible significant changes, examined their structural nature and questioned conventional predictions, thereby helping to identify signals of change and looking at reality in a different way.

By expressing ideas freely and exploring new ways of thinking in an open and creative environment, participants developed visions of the future that should enable the stakeholders to develop policy, to be innovative and to discover new ways of creating added value. To test the results of the scenarios, stakeholder days attended by eight sectors were held in autumn 2003. This process is ongoing, as the King Baudouin Foundation organises meetings at regional level. In February/March 2004, participants presented informed views of the problem, offering a better appreciation of the differences of opinion and proposals for further contact and joint actions between, for example, government, industry and their stakeholders.[27]

Strategy not only for the big shots

This chapter should not give the impression that only larger, traditional foundations can create value by taking on different roles. Quite the opposite is often true. Paying attention to the desired impact should drive the strategy, which can often be achieved without mobilising huge resources.

---

[27] http://www.kbs-frb.be

Promoting excellence in science

For example, The Novartis Foundation,[28] a scientific and educational charity formed in 1949 by the Swiss company Ciba (now Novartis), is funded with an annual donation from the company. The foundation, located in the heart of London's scientific community, aims to promote scientific excellence by convening scientific meetings, publishing books and communicating science to the public. In this way, it plays the role of convenor.

Eight symposia held annually bring together 25 to 30 leading scientists from around the world to discuss topics at the cutting edge of their field. Each topic is presented to an external peer review committee. The public is invited to attend one-day open meetings. Topics over the past decade include immunology, genetics, cell biology, developmental biology, molecular genetics and neurobiology. In addition, agricultural and environmental topics have been included in the programme and the published reports.

Preserving a movement

The small Thomas Neirynck Fund, hosted inside the King Baudouin Foundation, was created to bring together the works of the Cobra period, an art movement that began in Denmark and spread to Brussels and Amsterdam from 1935 to 1945. The donor, Thomas Neirynck, had collected more than 700 paintings by the time he turned 80. At the same time, the Brussels-based Bernheim Foundation was considering what to do with the bequeathal of a house. Contacts with a professor at The University of Brussels revealed that several other Cobra paintings

---

[28] http://www.novartisfound.org.uk

needed a home. The university created a museum in the Bernheim Foundation's house to display the collection.

In this instance, a charitable donation created a new situation, which spurred the fund as an agent of change to bring together different actors, thus fulfilling the role of convenor.

2

Responding to a changing policy environment

To fulfil their obligation to create value, foundations must fully understand the context in which they assume their various roles and how to best meet the economic, cultural, and social needs of the societies in which they work. Policy-makers and the public are calling for greater involvement by civil society, but to fulfil their obligations, foundations must take into consideration the policy environment in which they operate. In defining this environment, it is critical to evaluate the interplay of roles among the state, the market and civil society.

The roles of the state and civil society

Foundations are often expected to be "the voice of civil society" and, extrapolating from that role, could be viewed as custodians of democracy. To meet these expectations, practitioners must become more aware of the changes brought about in democratic states by the forces of globalisation and liberalisation. In a paper published by the Center for Democracy and the Third Sector at Georgetown University, the authors argue:

> While we take for granted that philanthropy is a force for change, we have not
> yet taken account of how philanthropy itself is being reshaped by social, politi-
> cal, demographic and economic changes in democratic states, both old and
> new; by the reorganisation of the arrangements that link the state to the third
> sector; by globalisation and the emergence of new transnational, regional, and
> local networks of social and political actors; or by changes in technology and in
> the organisation of firms.[1]

Today's accelerating pace of change raises a fundamental question
about the roles of the state and civil society and how they impact upon
the role of foundations. What happens when private foundations
based on the American model (referred to as Anglo-Saxon in this
chapter) export their philanthropy to western and eastern Europe?
Does this cookie-cutter approach work? Arguably, not very effectively
in societies were the state is not in retreat and citizens expect it to
deliver social services. How can foundations determine their various
roles in a policy environment that is constantly evolving?

To frame the debate for the US and Europe, this chapter considers
the role of the state, four models of civil society – Anglo-Saxon,
Rhine, Latin/Mediterranean and Scandinavian – and how the various
models impact upon the roles played by the foundations. It also makes
an argument that in light of these differences, there is a strong case for
foundations to continue to fulfil the role of catalysts for social and
political change, while evolving further into the role of convenor, as
an engaged member of civil society committed to laying the groundwork for informed policy and decision-making that is more inclusive.

The role of the state

The role of the state is a dynamic process, directly linked to social
traditions, economic changes and technological innovations. For

---

[1] *Doing Democracy's Work? The Transformation of Global Philanthropy in the Twentieth
Century,* Center for Democracy and the Third Sector, Georgetown University, October
2003, p. 4.

example, in Europe both the Renaissance and the Industrial Revolution brought about profound changes in the role of the state, which was previously a very simple one, whether it was a city-state or an empire. The Russian Revolution in 1917 created a new role for the state, based upon an ideological foundation of socialism and centrally planned economies. This was in sharp contrast to the democratic liberalism based on a free market economic system, freedom of the press and free and fair elections. The tension between these two roles escalated after World War II and lasted until the USSR began to disintegrate in 1991.

There has traditionally been a wide-ranging debate among politicians, academics, economists, entrepreneurs and activists about the role of the state in society and the economy. However, almost everyone agrees that the state has a role in providing primary education, health care, some physical infrastructure, governance (by way of law and order) and defence.

In recent years, this debate has intensified and burst into activism as the pressure of globalisation has led to a massive sweep of privatisation and liberalisation of markets. Witness the position taken by most trade unions and a good number of civil society activists, amplified in the recent past by the violence of anti-globalisation protestors. Consider as well the ongoing debate over the privatisation of public services such as waste treatment, water and electricity.

Is the state retreating?

Since World War II, Europe has been recognised as one of the most advanced societies in the world because economic and social progress have gone hand-in-hand and been mutually reinforcing. This vital link has taken different forms from country to country, but what is known as the European social model reflects the same set of values and produces comparable policies and institutions. This has been the backbone of European integration and is at the heart of the enlargement – or reintegration – of the EU from 15 to 25 members.

There is little doubt that European society as a whole is based more on collective solidarity than is American society. In Europe, a sense of collective solidarity has been achieved via an extended social security system. As a result, social cohesion has historically been viewed as the business of the state. Although the role of the state is rapidly changing for many reasons, primarily because of the forces of globalisation, privatisation and liberalisation, so too are the roles of the private sector and civil society.

Moves away from the model of the state as provider towards that of regulator have raised serious questions, with some accusing the state of retreating from its responsibilities, leaving the delivery of public services to the private sector. As a result, often ruthless market forces determine the level and quality of services that populations have come to expect from their governments. This is true in the US, perhaps, but arguably not to the same extent in Europe.

In western and northern Europe, the potential withdrawal of the state evokes deep historical dilemmas about the division of labour among government or public authorities, society and civil society. The paper by the Center for Democracy and the Third Sector at Georgetown University questions whether the deregulation of philanthropy in the USA is simply a way for the state to retreat from the task of building political communities grounded in egalitarian conceptions of national identity and citizenship among an increasingly heterogeneous population, or, whether it is a way for the state to withdraw from providing welfare. The paper further posits:

> Recent trends hold out the possibility that, together with the broader erosion of welfare regimes, Europe could be on the verge of a moment comparable to the American "philanthropic revolution" of the early 19th century, signalling significant shifts in large scale patterns of state–society relations.[2]

State spending on public services in several European countries (Figure 2.1) and the EU average disproves this theory, which is all-too-often

---

[2] Ibid, p. 11.

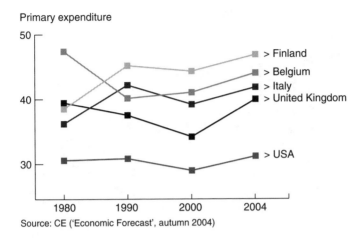

Source: CE ('Economic Forecast', autumn 2004)

Figure 2.1 Public administrations' expenses structure in a number of EU member states (% of GDP)

expressed at international fora. The numbers reveal that, in fact, state spending in several countries is either stable or on the increase (see Figures 2.2 and 2.3). In particular and contrary to public opinion, spending patterns in education and social services demonstrate that, overall, the reality in Europe is that the state is not retreating dramatically. Spending could be going down, but this could also be related to the nature of funding. For example, a museum's funding may appear to have been cut by public authorities, while in reality it has procured other sources of financial support.

Primary expenditure	1980	1990	2000	2004
> Finland	39.6	47.2	46.2	49.1
> Belgium	49.7	41.5	42.5	45.9
> Italy	37.0	43.8	40.4	43.4
> United Kingdom	40.7	38.5	34.7	41.3
> USA	30.6	30.9	28.8	31.3

Source: CE ('Economic Forecast', autumn 2004)

Figure 2.2 Public administrations' expenses structure in a number of EU member states (% of GDP)

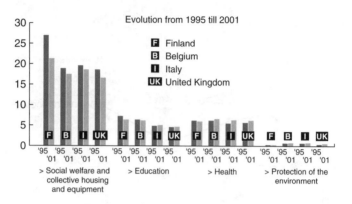

Figure 2.3 Public expenses by function (% of GNP)

In the US, however, a completely different reality prevails, which stands in sharp contrast to the European environment. Governor Arnold Schwarzenegger's first budget, presented January 2004, was based on a $76 billion spending plan for the state of California that includes significant cuts in health care, public education and payments to local governments. The Governor acknowledged that the reductions would be painful to many of the poorest Californians, but claimed that there was no other way to address the $14 billion deficit. This follows in the footsteps of US President George Bush, whose domestic policy includes deep tax cuts that critics claim are depriving America of the money it needs to address its deep-rooted problems – poverty, health care and education.

Understanding the policy environment is critical

This level of state expenditure on public services to a great extent defines the policy environment within which civil society and foundations act. More importantly, it reveals the amount of "space" available between the state and the market for civil society actors to carry out their activities. It is critical to understand this policy environment when foundations are assessing their strategies and methodologies.

Because foundations have an obligation to create value – indeed to take value creation to a different level – in the societies in which they operate, they must also understand the context in which civil society is operating. This is particularly true if indeed one of the roles of foundations is to foster pluralism and complementarity by compensating for democratic deficits and acting as the voice of civil society, as argued in Chapter 1. It is even more important when a foundation plays the roles of catalyst and convenor in an environment where the leverage point for real change is often at the public authority level, as it is in Europe.

In analysing the policy environment, the lines between public and private responsibilities are drawn differently in different societies and are sometimes blurred. At the same time, people are often ambivalent towards the state as they expect a certain level of social services and employment. However, they resent interference and over-regulation.

A paradox exists in central and eastern European countries, where the role of the state must be even stronger, as these fledgling democracies make the often-painful transition from centrally planned to market economies. This is because the success of this transition is dependent on good governance, as transparent and accountable governance is a foundation for sustainable development. Increasingly, trading partner countries and individual companies are demanding such governance, which includes respect for human rights and freedoms, democratic principles and the rule of law. Creating such an environment must involve a strong state and local authorities, with participation by civil society and all economic and social actors. For this reason, working exclusively with civil society organisations in these countries and ignoring the public authorities and other actors is short-sighted and does not lead to sustainable, long-term solutions.

The complexities of civil society

It is in this murky territory that civil society must find its voice and make itself heard. As argued throughout the literature, defining civil society is no easy task. In the introduction to a volume of studies examining civil society, editors Chris Hann and Elizabeth Dunn point out that their authors argue for a more inclusive usage of civil society, in which it is not defined negatively in opposition to the state but positively in the context of the ideas and practices through which cooperation and trust are established in social life.

> There are few places in the late 20th century world where the policies of the state and the actions of its agents in implementing them do not play a central role in these processes. These people, and the very idea of the state, should therefore be integrated into the analysis (of civil society) rather than bracketed outside it.[3]

Hann and Dunn point out that in western societies, primarily in the Anglo-Saxon model, civil society has been positioned as "a unified realm in opposition to the state, and that its recent reduction by governments and aid agencies (such as the World Bank and other international organisations) to the world of non-governmental organisations (NGOs) represents an impoverished view of social life".[4]

What is civil society?

As academics, theorists and philosophers ponder the definition of civil society and trace its origins from the eighteenth and nineteenth centuries, the Centre for Civil Society (CCS) at the London School of Economics recognises that "it is a concept located strategically at the cross-section of important strands of intellectual developments in the social sciences", and proffers the following as an initial working definition:

> Civil society refers to the set of institutions, organisations and behaviour situated between the state, the business world and the family. Specifically, this

---

[3] Chris Hahn and Elizabeth Dunn, *Civil Society, Challenging Western Models*, Routledge, 1996.
[4] Ibid.

includes voluntary and non-profit organisations of many different kinds, philanthropic institutions, social and political movements, other forms of social participation and engagement and the values and cultural patterns associated with them.[5]

CCS theorises that for the past 50 years, social scientists believed in a two-sector world – the market or economy on the one hand and the state or government on the other. The notion that a "third sector" might exist between the other two was lost in the two-sector view (see Figure 2.4). It also argues that such a shortsighted approach has resulted in "disastrous consequences" in terms of understanding how economies and societies interact, of which the inability of the social sciences to predict and understand the fall of communism in central and eastern Europe is just one example.

According to CCS: "For too long we have held a preconceived notion of 'the market' and 'the state' that were seemingly independent of local societies and cultures. The debate about civil society ultimately is about how culture, market and state relate to each other."[6]

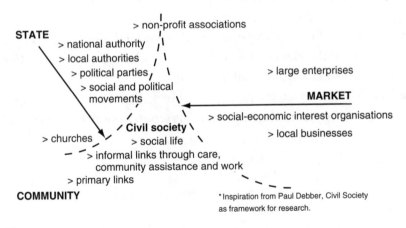

Figure 2.4   Threats civil society might have to face*

[5] Centre for Civil Society, *What is Civil Society?* London School of Economics, http://lse.acc.uk/collections/CCS/what_is_civil_society.htm.
[6] Ibid.

The International Network on Strategic Philanthropy (INSP) holds the view that the intellectual history of the term "civil society" is closely intertwined with the notion of citizenship, the limits of state power, and the foundation, as well as the regulation of market economies: "The prevailing modern view sees civil society as a sphere located between state and market – a buffer zone strong enough to keep both state and market in check, thereby preventing each from becoming too powerful and dominating."[7]

As such, civil society is not a singular, monolithic, separate entity, but a "sphere" constituted in relation to both state and market, and permeating both. This view is shared by Andrew Crook, CIVICUS in Europe,[8] who suggests in a working paper that civil society exists in the spaces or spheres of interaction between the state and political and economic society, and in important ways mediates between them. Crook maintains that differences between civil societies in the various European nations significantly reflect the size and shape of the spaces left available for civil society actors and their institutions. Facts that affect the size and shape of the spaces and the ability of civil society actors to make use of them include, but are not limited to:

- The degree to which the state remains powerful, centralised, and is regarded as the chief welfare provider and arbiter of public good (for example, in France and Finland).
- The degree to which the principle of subsidiarity[9] applies (for example, in Germany, where the state contracts services out to civil society).

---

[7] International Network on Strategic Philanthropy, *International Dictionary of Civil Society, Philanthropy, and Nonprofit Organizations*, UCLA School of Public Policy and Social Research, November 2003.

[8] Andrew Crook, *European Civil Society or Civil Society in Europe?* The sketch of a Working Paper for CIVICUS in Europe, www.civicusineurope.org. (CIVICUS: World Alliance for Citizen Participation is an international organisation dedicated to strengthening citizen action and civil society throughout the world. Its European Regional office is based in Budapest.)

[9] In the EU, subsidiarity is the principle whereby the Union does not take action (except in the areas that fall within its exclusive competence) unless it is more effective than action taken at national, regional or local level.

- The extent to which societies are organised around socio-political pillars of socialist and church institutions (for example, in Belgium and the Netherlands). In such societies, government and the church have tended to divide the provision of welfare between themselves, leaving relatively little space for "private" civil society organisations.
- The degree to which the nation has enjoyed social and political stability over a long period of time. (State building concentrates on achieving unity and uniformity and thus does not privilege civil society. Extreme left- or right-wing governments do their best to destroy it.)
- The existence of local power structures to which emerging civil society institutions can easily relate.
- The adequacy of civil society law and fiscal provisions (for example, the presence or absence of mortmain).
- The degree of cooperation/distrust between government/public authorities and civil society actors and institutions.
- The degree of economic development and the availability of indigenous public and private funding.

Is there a European model of civil society?

This question could be answered by a tentative "yes", insofar as there is a truly European culture and identity. William Outhwaite of the University of Sussex asks how far can one discern the beginnings of a European civil society "which is more than just the sum of civil societies in Europe". He quotes French sociologist Henri Mendras in answering the question, "What is distinctive about European modernity?":

> This model is made up of ideological innovations: the individualist idea of man; the distinction between three types of legitimacy: religious, political and economic; the notion of capital; the combination of science and technology, the power of the majority; the binding force of contract and of the relation of trust which

it presupposes; the constitutional state and Roman property law. These are the fundamental elements of western European civilisation, which are unique in the history of civilisation.[10]

Outhwaite postulates that despite the Americanising pull of the mass media, Europe will remain culturally distinct from other world regions, with local differences persisting against a background of common European and global systems. But he does recognise that Europe is an entity with "fuzzy edges", both externally (some European states include Overseas Territories and Countries and both Turkey and Russia stretch into Asia) and internally. Traditional divisions are shifting in dramatic ways. He writes:

> It is not just that the old political east/west division has now been replaced by an economic one. The cultural north/south divide within Europe, marked for example by the line between potatoes and pasta, remains important, but is changing in many ways, with the modernisation of (parts of the) southern European societies. It is now for example Italy, rather than the Protestant northern countries, which (in the absence of adequate child care provision) apparently puts work before having children.
>
> The north–south religious divide remains an important structural principle in western Europe, as does, further east, that between Orthodox Christianity and Islam. The east–west line also remains crucial, as Germans on both sides (but especially the east) will confirm, and many central Europeans would also continue to stress the distinctiveness of their societies from "eastern" Europe as well as from Russia. There are also many similarities between Scandinavia and parts of east central Europe, despite their diverse political histories for much of the 20th century.[11]

These divisions are important to understanding the different models of civil society. Hann and Dunn argue for a "need to shift

---

[10] William Outhwaite, "Toward a European civil society?" Published in *The Shape of the New Europe*, Cambridge University Press, March 2004, p. 6.
[11] Ibid, p. 8.

the debates about civil society away from formal structures and organisations and towards an investigation of beliefs, values and everyday practices".[12]

Cultural paradigms die hard

These beliefs, values and everyday practices are still very much entrenched in the past. In reality, despite the forces of secularisation and postmodernism, cultural paradigms die hard, which accounts in part for the different civil society models within Europe. Foundations must take these diversities into account in their work if they want to be effective in creating real value.

Consider that for the most part southern European society is still characterised by a very Catholic paradigm, in which moral education is more a social phenomenon with a collective conscience. Values are learned through the group, which explains why more importance is given to social groups (even classes in the past). Social cohesion is an essential part of the fabric of the society. This is rooted in the fact that, in Catholicism, the moral authority and responsibility is vertically organised: the Pope has a direct relationship with God, from which he gets the "truth" that is subsequently passed down through priests to the individual.

Protestant ethics dominate in northern Europe, where moral education is individual, based on personal experience and judgement. A Protestant priest is *primus inter pares*, as he assists the faithful in achieving the ultimate aim of an individual conscience that is shaped by religious principles.

This dynamic is manifested in a myriad of ways across Europe. For example, the *ex cathedra* (authoritative) method of teaching is prevalent in the south. In Protestant cultures, students and teachers tend to

---

[12] Ibid, p. 14.

work with hands on cases and examples; questioning, debating and discussing is the norm.

In health care, these differences manifest themselves in approaches to individual health. In a Catholic culture, there tends to be a more passive or curative attitude rather than a preventative one towards individual health. In Protestant cultures, there is more of a sense of personal responsibility for one's health.

Such divergent approaches have consequences on health care systems, but also on the work of organisations in their approaches to poverty reduction. In the south, the structural reasons for poverty are addressed, while in the north, the individual responsibility of the poor is also put on the table for discussion. In the north, such differences have a methodological impact, as donors tend more towards individual scholarships and grants; in the south, there is a stronger focus on project funding.

In this context, civil society is quite a different animal in the north than it is in the south as it is responding to very different realities and cultural paradigms. It follows that foundations can – and do – play a role in building and servicing civil society. But their work depends on and reflects the differentiations of the societies in which they operate. Differences in attitudes towards the roles of the state, the private sector, civil society and the individual have a profound impact on the way foundations conduct their business.

Models of civil society

Parallel to this is the question of how these differences will persist in the future against the backdrop of globalisation of both economic and managerial structures. However, today three models can be identified across Europe, outside of the Anglo-Saxon model: the Rhine, the Latin/Mediterranean and the Scandinavian. These models are evolving and changing, as are the societies, but distinctive characteristics can be identified. The models described in this chapter are generalisations only. Some may overlap or a civil society may be a hybrid of several.

This reality defies the standardised methodological approaches sometimes taken by foundations. This approach cannot see past the Anglo-Saxon model, prevalent in the US and, for the most part, in the UK. Because foundations are viewed as being an integral part of civil society, the particular civil society model they are working within determines the roles it fulfils and the methodologies they use.

The Anglo-Saxon model

Hann and Dunn maintain that civil society in Britain differs in important ways from that in America and that there is no single contemporary western model.[13] In fact, there exists an Anglo-Saxon model, which could be applied in various degrees to both the US and the UK. Crook describes it as characterised by ancient roots and unbroken history, very well established and non-political; extensive and involving free cooperation with public authorities.[14]

In these societies, civil society organisations are viewed as being a counterweight to government and the state. In an ideal situation, they fulfil a complementarity function in fostering pluralism and cast themselves in the roles of critics of the state and advocates of reform.

---

[13] Ibid, p. 12.

[14] Andrew Crook, *European Civil Society or Civil Society in Europe?* The sketch of a Working Paper for CIVICUS in Europe, www.civicusineurope.org. (CIVICUS: World Alliance for Citizen Participation is an international organisation dedicated to strengthening citizen action and civil society throughout the world. Its European Regional office is based in Budapest.)

It is in the democratic state's interest to have a strong civil society sector. This is reflected in the legal and fiscal infrastructure, which creates an environment involving a tax treatment that favours and encourages donations and gifts. There is also a strong culture of volunteerism, which is weaker in other countries. In this space, foundations play the roles fostering complementarity and pluralism by supporting civil society and funding those issues that governments do not.

The Rhine model

In this model, which includes Belgium, Germany and the Netherlands, there are strong civil society organisations that are institution-like and often receive contracts from the state; it is a form of societal corporatism. For example, in sectors such as health care and education, they function much like subcontractors. Paradoxically, they are independent from the state, but almost 100% publicly financed. Historically, they are organised in ideological pillars, such as socialist, liberal, or Christian Democrat. The citizen chooses where to receive services, which creates competition and, hence, efficiency. In this situation, professional civil society organisations are an organic part of the welfare state system.

Manuel Pérez Yruela writes,

> An organisational network is...created that participates with the state in the management of public policies and services. This network has come to create an institutional system of collaboration between the state and civil society. Although it is still difficult and confusing to define, it could be labelled the "private management of public interests".[15]

Because of the interdependent relationship and dependency on government funding, the fiscal and legal climate does not strongly favour

---

[15] Manuel Pérez Yruela, *Corporatism and Civil Society*, Instituto de Estudios Sociales de Andalucia, Córdoba.

donations and gifts. In this space, foundations are only recently being recognised as important players, particularly corporate foundations. For example, in Germany, the major foundations are linked to corporations, such as Bosch, Volkswagen and Bertelsmann.

The Latin/Mediterranean model

In these countries the role of the state has traditionally been strong. Since Napoleonic times there has been a clear division between church and state – traditionally the church does charity work and the state is responsible for delivering the goods and social services to its citizens. The state is also a strong economic actor, although in recent years, the wave of privatisation and liberalisation is changing this dynamic. However, it is unlikely that citizens will support privatisation of services they view as universal, such as health care, education, and in some cases, transportation. In this socioeconomic model the relationship between the state and market is different from that in the Anglo-Saxon model, which distinguishes continental Europe from the US and, to a large extent, the UK.

In this model, civil society organisations face a challenge in being accepted as independent and autonomous. There is a persistence to control organisations and associations politically, either through representations on the boards or by legal measures, such as what happened in Italy with the attempt to bring the banking foundations under political control (see page 49).

Gifts and donations are not strongly promoted by the fiscal system. Volunteerism is viewed as a threat to the job market, particularly by trade unions that oppose this type of activity in the health care and education sectors. Foundations are challenged to reach beyond their complementarity role because when they move into political territory, politicians who claim they do not have a mandate to act quickly challenge them.

The Scandinavian model

Traditionally, the state plays a strong role in these countries, but because of their Protestant roots, personal initiative is viewed as a positive. There is a dominant welfare state but, at the same time, volunteerism is a powerful force. Civil society organisations thrive and fulfil a complementary role to bridge the gaps in the system. Civil society often identifies the need, which is later filled by government.

Gifts and donations are not strongly promoted by the fiscal system. In this environment, foundations have a very strong relationship with government and government agencies.

Countries in transition

Eastern European countries are in the process of building and strengthening their civil societies. Donors, the EU, NGOs and western organisations such as the World Bank view this process as critical to strengthening democracy, improving governance and creating market economies. But as Hann and Dunn warn, civil society debates have been "too narrowly circumscribed by modern western models of liberal individualism". They point to the "errors and dangers" of exporting models of civil society to non-western societies:

> Millions of Eastern Europeans, and not just a few former communist *apparatchiks*, have now shown in elections that they wish to preserve some of the radical changes which took place in their societies under socialism. They do not accept that the new elites have a monopoly of the moral high ground, since there is little evidence in either eastern or western countries that the *laissez-faire* prescriptions of those who equate the rhetoric of "natural development" with that of "market economy" can enable the majority of citizens to realise (Czech Republic President Vaclav) Havel's romantic and Utopian ideals.[16]

---

[16] Ibid, p. 8.

The overall picture of the 10 additional member states of the European Union (EU) is one of significant convergence with the rest of the EU in terms of competitiveness, industrial structures and trade specialisation. They have achieved macroeconomic stability and offer generally liberalised markets and a climate of transparency and predictability for investors. Most have stable and relatively low inflation levels and have attracted significant levels of foreign investment. All of these factors have helped to restructure their enterprise sectors.

But at what cost? This has often been a painful transition, as the state is redefining its social commitments to conform with the EU's *acquis communautaire*[17] and create strong market economies. As a result, the nature of civil society and the role of foundations will reflect these fundamental shifts, as they are both still discovering the space they can occupy and roles they will be allowed to play in the future.

Civil society models and the work of foundations

The role of the state and its relationship to civil society defines the context in which foundations pursue their goals and has a profound impact on their work. Consider the impact that volunteerism – and the absence of it – carries with it, or the fact that community foundations, very popular in the US and the UK, are not being formed as quickly in continental Europe. The Italian court ruling in October 2003 marked a victory for foundations, but the fact that the government tried to curtail their independence is evidence that the environment for civil society, and thus the work of foundations, in that country within the Latin/Mediterranean model, is much different from other regions (see page 43).

---

[17] The *acquis communautaire* is the detailed laws and rules adopted on the basis of the EU's founding treaties.

Volunteerism: not necessarily the right thing to do

Volunteerism is a way of life in the US and the UK. In the 1980s, when US President Ronald Reagan called on Americans to volunteer in the health and education sectors – he called them "a thousand points of light" – what he was actually doing in his style of new federalism was calling on civil society to fill in the gaps left in the wake of a retreating state. He shifted dozens of federal programmes to the state and local levels, which were ill equipped and underfunded. Deregulation became the slogan for the Reagan administration, despite outcries from critics and civil society organisations warning that reduced regulation created hazards to public health and safety. This tradition, however, still continues under the Bush administration. America's "thousand points of light" have a lot of work to do.

Talking to a colleague in France or French-speaking Belgium about this trend and the resultant push towards volunteerism draws a blank stare. This attitude reflects the Latin/Mediterranean model, whereby the state is solely responsible for delivering social services, particularly health care and education. Government at all levels – from local and regional to national – must guarantee that these essential services can be funded from state coffers. This issue is also viewed through the lens of social cohesion, the need to build up human capital, and the fact that employment is considered to be the major integrating factor in society.

In this context, volunteerism is viewed as evidence of state failure and is accused of eroding social cohesion. Volunteers are taking paid jobs away from the labour market. There are some exceptions in the field of sports and in political action. Scepticism is also rooted in the fact that these societies are Catholic. In the past, the church was responsible for charity, which included delivering social services.

It would seem that foundations seeking to promote volunteerism in any sector in these countries are facing an uphill battle.

Donor-driven community foundations

Community foundations pool revenues and assets donated from a variety of sources and target action at community or neighbourhood level in a specific geographical region. Typically donor-driven, they are very popular in the US and are touted to be the fastest growing segment of the philanthropy field in Europe.

Roger M. Williams, writing in *Foundation News & Commentary*, refers to them as a growth industry.[18] The EFC reports that there are almost 100 community foundations across western Europe (three quarters of them are in the UK and Germany), and single examples in Portugal, Spain, Belgium, Ireland and Holland. They are being created in several eastern European countries, including the Czech Republic, Slovakia, Hungary, Bulgaria, Romania and the Baltic states. Williams maintains that the reasons behind this "boom" vary, but some are common to most of the countries:

- A new appreciation of the value of focusing philanthropy locally.
- A willingness to make it less a one-shot reaction than a planned, ongoing programme.
- Revised tax laws that make the formation of a community foundation easier and financially advantageous.
- A concept that promotes an overarching vision of what Europeans call community philanthropy, of which foundations are only one part.

American community foundations "really do work" according to Williams, who quotes William S. White, President of the (American) Charles Stewart Mott Foundation: "They give voice to the citizenry and to the idea that a community doesn't need some outside funder to parachute in with money." Mott exported the community foundation model to the UK in the 1980s and has been expanding the

---

[18] Roger M. Williams, "European growth industry", *Foundation News & Commentary*, September/October 2003, p. 40.

London-based Charities Aid Foundation initiative (a technical assistance programme for emerging community foundations) into 10 other countries with a total expenditure of $19.1 million in Europe.

The objective is also to "wean fledgling community foundation enthusiasts in eastern Europe away from dependence on the United States by giving them a place to go to in western Europe".

Williams rightly points out that the chief differences between European and American community foundations fall into the areas of endowment, tax burdens and marketing – that is, the solicitation of donor funds. But it is exactly these differences that could jeopardise the fate of European community foundations. Why should Europeans donate money that is already heavily taxed to a community foundation that is essentially doing – actually replacing – what should be the work of the state?

This type of philanthropy works well in the UK, which falls within the Anglo-Saxon model. But it should prove interesting, for example, to monitor the fate of the Community Foundation of Central and West Flanders, set up in 2002 by Levi Strauss Europe. In the wake of a manufacturing plant closure the company contacted local government and trades unions and offered to set up a community foundation. The locals accepted and the King Baudouin Foundation was asked to participate.

The first grants were redistributed to innovative grassroots projects set up by individuals in the fields of recreation, sports, play and leisure for youth and the elderly. A total of €93 795 has been redistributed to a total of 28 projects for 2002 and 2003. The objective for the future is to match Levi's seed money of $750 000. In 2004, local and regional businesses were approached to support the foundation, but whether or not they will participate remains to be seen.

In 2004, the Belgian media group Het Belang van Limburg, with its popular daily newspaper, decided to take a leadership role in getting donors involved in a new, creative community foundation. This could prove to be an effective instrument to reach out to donors in the Limburg region.

In Germany, the successful community foundations are often dependent on very few – and sometimes a single – inspired donors. Today, their boards and staff, most of whom are volunteers, work hard to attract multiple donors to match these original gifts. The outcome of their efforts over the mid to long term remains to be seen. In the UK, community foundations are channelling government funds as well as private donor contributions.

At a meeting of the Transatlantic Community Foundation Fellowship in July 2004, participants discussed how to keep the dynamics of community foundations going, particularly in Europe, where the issue of sustainability was raised. American participants expressed concern that certain European foundations were run almost exclusively by volunteers and by boards with weak management and organisational skills, which often results in less professionalism and, as a result, hinders their ability to attract donors.

The sustainability of the community foundation field goes beyond financial issues. For many years, US funders have been giving grants to community foundations in Europe; however, this funding is slowly drawing to an end. Now, more than ever, the European community foundation sector is relying on local donations to sustain their future development. At the outset, it was believed that through community work and playing a local leadership role, community foundations could create enough trust to generate local donations. In reality, this has not yet taken place enough. Old cultural paradigms die hard.

Italian banking foundations maintain their independence

In Italy there are about 90 banking foundations, with total assets in excess of €50 billion. They control more than 20 banks and have a strong influence on others. The foundations were created by the Amato banking reform of 1990 as temporary vehicles aimed at a rapid transformation of savings and public law banks. The Berlusconi government was determined to make a final break in the link between foundations and banks by turning foundations into charitable organisations that would be required to sell their bank shares within five years. The government introduced reform measures in 2001 as an amendment to the Finance Bill.

Under the new rules, the majority of seats on the boards of foundations were to go to representatives of local authorities. The foundations were to devote their activity to public causes, such as the arts, medicine and science, and allocate to their chosen cause at least 50% of their annual income. No bank, insurance or finance company executive would sit on the board of the foundations. Despite fierce opposition from many foundations and the political controversy that this move ignited, the amendment was approved. However, in September 2003, the Italian Constitutional Court declared that some of the changes to the law were unconstitutional.

This ruling strengthened the position of Italian foundations and reaffirmed their independence. During the run up to the reform, the EFC argued:

> The changes in the law undermined the independence of foundations of banking origin, thereby affecting their capacity to act for the social and economic develop-ment, well-being and progress of their communities, at local, regional and European levels.[19]

This move came as a shock to the Italian banking foundations, but it does conform to the characteristics of the Latin/Mediterranean model of civil society pertaining to the role of the state and foundations within that context. Some politicians were concerned that founda-tions would not be viewed as accountable, and therefore credible, unless they were controlled through democratically elected local or regional political representatives.

The EFC welcomes the confirmation of the key principle of founda-tions' independence by the Italian Constitutional Court. It also maintains that the ruling represents a victory for all foundations in Europe for their independence. It should, however, serve as a warning: foundations may be inviting government scrutiny and eventual regulation.

---

[19] European Foundation Centre, http://www.efc.be/content/alert.asp?ContentID=544.

A defining context

It is important for foundations to recognise and evaluate the policy environment in which they operate because they are considered to be a vital component of civil society. It is particularly essential that they understand the models within which they work and acknowledge that, within one country, there could be a hybrid of the various models discussed in this chapter.

Foundations play a number of roles simultaneously, from simple charity to the more complex role of catalyst of social and/or policy change. A fundamental responsibility is to create value, but as our societies become even more complex, the role of foundations as convenors emerges as one that will increasingly prevail. However, the degree to which they can fulfil their role as convenors will depend on whether foundations are viewed by both the political and corporate worlds as independent, accountable and credible organisations. It will also depend-able on whether civil society is recognised as having an organic, autonomous role.

As engaged members of civil society committed to laying the groundwork for informed policy and decision-making that is more inclusive, foundations can both fulfil their obligations and increase their social legitimacy. To accomplish this, they need to reach beyond grant-making and strive for sustainable impact.

3

Reaching beyond grant-making

Foundations, obligated to create value for the societies in which they operate, strive to accomplish this goal in many ways. However, the bottom line question for all donors is: "What is the most effective use of our funds?" Books and articles addressing this fundamental issue have been written over the years, but the mantra flowing through the literature concerns more effective grant-making, rather than moving beyond grant-making to embracing a broad spectrum of methodologies. The relatively "new" concept of a venture capital approach to philanthropy is also being held up as a way forward, particularly in the US.

Chapter 1 argued that foundations operating in sophisticated societies move through a broad band of often-overlapping roles, from charity and simple service delivery to strategic philanthropy and into the new role of convenor. If the mandate of a foundation is to solve, or even help to solve, complex social problems, it is essential to reach beyond the grant-making or operational mode into the role of convenor. In this way, the stakeholders as well as the wider community become engaged and the foundation's real value-added ends up falling somewhere in between the territory of catalyst and capacity builder.

A compendium of interviews with foundation executives, *Raising the Value of Philanthropy*, reports that if it is to make a difference, a foundation should act systematically to strategically deploy all available resources. One of the interviewees in its survey noted: "The traditional dependence solely on grant-making in achieving foundation goals may be the single biggest liability in the field of philanthropy." The report also notes that making the assumption that grant-making is the sole or principal way of doing business influences everything a foundation does. This in turn "perpetuates the imbalance of power" between the foundation and applicants and grantees, which may make it impossible to form meaningful partnerships, which are essential if one is to make progress in addressing complex social problems.[1]

A consensus is emerging that, in many instances, it is necessary to move beyond such a traditional paternalistic model if foundations are going to successfully fulfil any of their various roles. Several authors refer to "social justice philanthropy", which they maintain cannot be achieved by grant-making alone. To address issues of social justice, donors must deploy a wider range of tools, such as loans, which encourage communities to be more creative and productive through the discipline of borrowing and repayment. Some point to foundations' "convening role, when they use their clout and credibility to draw attention to issues, which can be more crucial than the funds they provide".[2]

It is time to shift the debate about whether foundations should be grant-making or operational, active or proactive (some prefer to label themselves as "responsive"), to how they can become more effective, strategic actors and value-added partners in their communities and, in some instances, on the world stage. To do this, foundations must understand the actions, or combination of actions, that are most likely to achieve their desired goals, and this, in turn, implies an understanding of the dynamics of change.

---

[1] Denis. J. Prager, *Raising the Value of Philanthropy. A synthesis of Informal Interviews with Foundation Executives and Observers of Philanthropy*, Jewish Healthcare Foundation, the Forbes Fund, and Grantmakers in Health, February 1999, p. 10.

[2] Andrew Milner, "Change or charity?" *Alliance*, Volume 8, Number 3, p. 23

What is wrong with the status quo?

The answer to this question is: "Plenty". It is almost a contradiction in terms for a foundation to strive to maintain the status quo as many strive ultimately to effect meaningful social and political change in their quest to improve the lives of citizens and the world we live in. In many instances, foundations have outgrown their roles as grant-makers and are moving into different spheres of action, underpinned by programming that they believe reflects their role – or roles – in society.

In a paper delivered at The Hague Club Meeting[3] in 1998, Victor de Sá Machado[4] distinguishes between three types of foundation – those following a methodology of granting funds (the reactive foundation), foundations that act directly (active or operational, selecting the intervention sectors and implementing under their responsibility and guidance the means to materialise initiatives of their own), and mixed foundations that do both. This categorisation sheds some light on the structural relationship between foundations and the societies they serve and strengthens the notion that foundations should act "with a view to reinforce the society itself from which they stem". Ultimately, however, the author argues that in both strong and weak societies, "foundations are meant to serve the society for which they work… their ultimate purpose is to contribute to a more participated, more engaged and more committed society".

In some cases, the thorny politics of grant-making, pushed by an increasing public demand to be transparent and accountable, could cause foundations to act in a shortsighted manner, focusing only on programmes and actions that result in tangible, measurable outcomes. Prager maintains that this results in the important being crowded out by the immediate. In his view, this situation reflects the "tyranny of

---

[3] The Hague Club is a private association of major independent European foundations.
[4] Victor de Sá Machado, former president of The Gulbenkian Foundation, Portugal, *Foundations: Active or Reactive*, 1998, p. 5.

the grant cycle". Another noxious side-effect is the power imbalance, which one interviewee labelled "a serious co-dependency problem", whereby communities become dependent upon external forces (foundations) and resources to solve their problems, and those external forces measure their effectiveness by how much they have contributed to solving them.[5]

Would it not be better to focus on capacity-building, stimulating sustainable social and political change and building stronger self-supporting communities capable of mobilising themselves? (In this instance, "communities" is used in its broader sense, which also refers to communities of interest, or stakeholders, as well as local, regional, national or global communities.)

Creative grant-making is advocated by Ruth Tebbets Brousseau as a way to improve the status quo. She draws upon interviews with 10 recipients of the (US) Council on Foundations' Scrivner Award, given annually to honour the work of a grant-maker selected as an exemplar of creativity in philanthropy. Five common themes most central to creative grant-making were identified, which she calls "the foundations of creativity" – a motivating belief, a range of cognitive skills, interpersonal competence, crossing boundaries and mixing worlds, and a sense of journey. When "crossing boundaries and mixing worlds", Brousseau reports that Scrivner awardees often crossed many different social and cultural boundaries, working individually and in groups with people and organisations occupying very different roles and places in the social order.[6]

This type of activity moves the grant-maker or the foundation closer to the roles of catalyst of social and political change and convenor, which requires a healthy, calculated, well-managed balance of methodologies and strategies.

---

[5] Ibid, p. 15.
[6] Ruth Tebbets Brousseau, "Experienced grantmakers at work", *When Creativity Comes Into Play*, The Foundation Center, January 2004, p. 5.

Proactive vs reactive: striking a balance

The distinction among the classification of foundations as active, proactive, reactive, responsive, grant-making or operational, is blurred for those who define their roles in terms of instigating social and/or political change or as a convenor. It is worth exploring the various labels and tensions among them as they depict the underlying motivation for foundations and often describe their relationships with communities and civil society.

Proactive grant-making, as described by Prager, is motivated by the desire to take the initiative in defining how social problems will be addressed, and to be innovative in generating such initiatives. Reactive grant-making is the more traditional awarding of grants in response to unsolicited proposals. The advantage of proactive grant-making is that it gives the foundation the sense that it is using its resources in a coherent and integrated manner. "From the point of view of organisations struggling to address a particular social problem through service delivery, advocacy, education, or research, proactive grant-making seems to be yet another attempt to raise the bar over which organisations must jump in order to receive support needed to sustain their operations," he writes. The worst case scenario is that it leads to resentment, whereby organisations perceive foundations as "top down" and arrogant. Equally dangerous is the fear that the growing tendency towards proactive grant-making will result in increased isolation of foundation staff from the "real world" where problems exist and those working on the ground are trying to solve them.[7]

Tom David, Executive Vice-President of the California Wellness Foundation, argues for the virtues of both, but prefers the term "responsive" to reactive. As to which mode is most strategic for a particular foundation, he notes that the answer depends on three interrelated

---

[7] Ibid, p. 3.

factors: its mission, its values and operational philosophy and the developmental stage of the organisation. In describing a spectrum of strategic approaches, he notes that "responsive" refers to foundations that emphasise connectedness to local needs and priorities as defined and articulated by grant-seekers themselves.

The spectrum moves from responsive to proactive through strategic approaches covering the following dimensions – community based, priority focused, capacity building, research and development, active partnership and purveyor of information (Figure 3.1). The ultimate goal for this particular foundation is to implement and explore the consequences of a grant-making portfolio that aims for dynamic balance across several dimensions. David explains that in the health care "marketplace", no single static strategy is likely to prove successful no matter how creative it may appear.[8]

In a second paper delivered at The Hague Club Meeting in 1998, Anthony Tomei[9] describes active funding, whereby a foundation is actively involved in the conduct of a project. The advantages lie in the fact that it ensures that the project is being properly managed and also brings the foundation's expertise, networks and added value into play. He notes that while responsive funding may be "rather

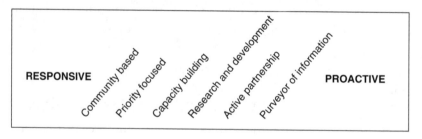

Figure 3.1   A spectrum of strategic approaches to grant-making

---

[8] Tom David, "Reflections on strategic grantmaking", *The California Wellness Foundation*, Volume 2, Number 1, November 2000, p. 3.
[9] Anthony Tomei, Director, Nuffield Foundation, *Foundations – Active or Reactive?* September 1998, pp. 4–6.

unfashionable", it also generates advantages. The first concerns the very nature and role of foundations: while they have an important part to play in bringing about social change and improvement, they are rarely themselves the direct agents of that change.

"Their role, rather, is to identify creative and talented individuals in their fields of interest and to support their work," he writes. Tomei draws a comparison with the world of publishing. It is the publisher's job to bring a range of skills and expertise to the business of bringing the written word to the reading public. These skills include editing, marketing, design and, above all, the ability to recognise and encourage talented writers. Publishers do not write novels.

He also points to the fact that foundations derive their legitimacy from the fact that they do not hold particular views and see themselves as "honest brokers". There is danger that foundations and funders in general may become "too prescriptive" about the nature of the work they fund: "Too narrow a definition of a problem area will close down debate too early." Finally, modes of funding that are too prescriptive could stifle a defining characteristic of foundations, which is their freedom to support the unexpected, the unorthodox and to fill in gaps in their societies.

Tomei argues for striking the right balance: "The issue is to find ways of managing grant programmes that combine the best of both." He cautions that there is no general model for promoting social change. What is ultimately important is that the foundation has an idea of what it wants to achieve and a realistic sense of what it can do to help.

Although this is a valid argument, there is a case to be made for leaving this neutral ground for a more engaged type of convenor or "honest broker" type of role.

Framing the debate, setting an example

The UK-based Nuffield Foundation, a charitable trust established in 1943, funds research and practical work in social policy, education and science.

Foundation Trustees established The Nuffield Council on Bioethics[10] in 1991 as an independent body to consider the ethical issues arising from developments in medicine and biology. The Council is funded jointly by the Nuffield Foundation, The Wellcome Trust and the Medical Research Council.

It plays a major role in contributing to policy-making and stimulating debate in the controversial field of bioethics. In this way, it perfectly fulfils the role of foundation as convenor, through deploying the methodologies of creating a think tank and engaging in advocacy. Once the Council has identified a topic for investigation, it establishes a multidisciplinary group with the relevant expertise to examine and report on the issue. Topics covered range from genetic screening, human tissue, animal-to-human transplants and genetically modified crops, to the ethics of patenting DNA and pharmacogenetics.

Because genetic research differs from many areas of medical R&D, and because of its profound effect on individuals, their families and society in general, the Nuffield Council decided to make genetic screening the subject of its first report.

Genetic screening for diseases such as cystic fibrosis and sickle cell anaemia raises key ethic, legal and practical issues. A Working Party established in 1991 examined such issues as consent to being screened, counselling, the risk of stigma, confidentiality, possible use of genetic information by insurers or employers, and the storage and use of genetic information for legal purposes.

The report, published in 1993, was recognised as setting the agenda for public and political discussion on human genetics. It recommended that the voluntary nature of all screening programmes should be emphasised and that adequately informed consent be a requirement. It also suggested that a central coordinating body be established to monitor genetic screening programmes. The report's conclusions

---

[10] http://www.nuffieldbioethics.org

have been widely endorsed and many of the themes identified are still the subject of public debate.

Nuffield Foundation Director, Anthony Tomei, says that the foundation established the Council on Bioethics when it learned that the government had decided not to establish its own source of advice on important bioethics questions.

"As time has passed, the advantages of having an independent, rather than a government body in this controversial field have become increasingly apparent," he says. "The government is now considering setting up a national bioethics commission. We want to persuade them not to lose the advantage of our model."

A broad spectrum of methodologies

Reaching beyond grant-making, in whatever form, embraces a broad spectrum of methodologies in many combinations, depending on the issues that are being tackled. They run the gamut from public education, advocacy, publications, seminars, and think tanks to advocacy and communication campaigns in tandem with proactive grant-making. Authors write about the strategic deployment of resources and competences, but most important is an understanding of the leverage points of change and how a foundation can best mobilise its resources to exercise them.

Ralph R. Smith, Senior Vice-President at the Annie Casey Foundation (Baltimore, USA), says, "there is no doubt...that non-grant activities allow us to achieve results that otherwise would not be possible." For example, advocacy work or working as a broker to settle irreconcilable differences between interest groups, such as his foundation's role in reforming the child welfare system in New York City, could not have succeeded if the foundation was restricted to grant-making:

This is the kind of work that is not amenable to just a grant. The institutional credibility we lent to the effort, the hands-on involvement of senior Casey staff, and the network of experts we were able to draw on – all this mattered at least as much as the flexible dollars we provided.[11]

Prager calls this "solving problems from the inside out rather than from the outside in", based on the belief that "communities have the capacity to act as communities in addressing problems they perceive to be of high priority". If empowered to do so, communities can organise themselves strategically to take on major problems by working together in a communal way. For foundations that embrace this belief, it means that the principal focus of their efforts to address community issues is catalysing, facilitating and supporting efforts by communities to pull together to:

- Define their needs and priorities.
- Establish the goals they wish to achieve and the timeframe in which they hope to achieve them.
- Figure out how to work together in such a way as to make a real difference in the quality of life of the community in which they live.
- Decide the kind of help they need from the outside.

Foundations adopting this "alternative paradigm" require a whole new way of thinking. Instead of defining what they think represents the most important problems facing communities, their role is to help communities to think more strategically about the future and to mobilise community resources in such a way that they not only contribute to the solution of today's specific problems, but can then be used to address tomorrow's problems.[12]

---

[11] Les Silverman, "Building better foundations", The McKinsey Quarterly, Number 1, 2004, p. 98.
[12] Ibid, p. 16.

The Architectural Heritage Programme

This dynamic drove the King Baudouin Foundation's (KBF) Flanders Architectural Heritage Programme, the success of which depended on engaging a broad range of stakeholders, including the government, local public authorities and citizens organisations (NGOs). The project deployed a strategic mix of methodologies in an initiative that started 20 years ago. Its dynamism still lives on, despite KBF's withdrawal of financial support in 1998.

The King Baudouin Foundation has been devoting its attention to architectural heritage since it was founded more than 25 years ago. Its attention to the preservation of Belgium's architectural heritage was an expression of KBF's broader interest in quality of life, such as town and country planning and the environment.

This initiative represented a long-term commitment, whereby the foundation engaged in a multitude of roles and deployed a broad spectrum of methodologies to carry out specific projects and to engage both citizens and the public sector in its activities. In some instances it acted hands-on and in others it simply provided the funding. The result was that the heritage sector, which had been fragmented and the purview of the few, was galvanised and is still thriving and moving forward without direct KBF involvement.

In 1982, the foundation published a *White Paper for Cultural Movable Heritage*, which revealed that Belgium had dropped substantially behind most of the other European Union countries. It also revealed that most countries had implemented legislation and regulations in areas that supported and maintained the preservation of their architectural heritage, such as tax deductions, low interest loans and inheritance regulations. The paper also set out concrete ways to better protect Belgium's heritage.

One year later, these ideas were put into action with support from the National Lottery, which kick-started the first restoration projects. The first amount from the Lottery of €743 681, increased in 1987 to €1.11 million and one year later to €1.85 million.

Creating a multiplier effect

The 15-year Architectural Heritage Programme was designed around three pillars: structure, awareness and assistance. As such, it was focused on long-term capacity building and resulted in concrete restoration projects, public awareness activities and an engaged sector, as heritage professionals worked together for monuments to be opened to the public in a socially integrated way (Open Monuments Day). A multiplier effect was created through supporting projects and increasing awareness among the population and policy-makers.

In practice, restoration campaigns began in earnest in 1983 and continued until 1993, involving local, and in many cases, unprotected heritage buildings. "Associations working to save our monuments" (1985–1988) and "Monuments – something we care about" (1991–1993) were highly successful programmes, supported by a wide range of publications, monument visits, seminars and information days. Young people attended excavation camps and the work branched out into a discovery of Belgium's industrial archaeological heritage.

Over the life of the programme dozens of projects were approved and supported. This experience on the ground, together with research and study carried out for the related publications, earned the Architectural Heritage Programme a solid reputation and with its recognised expertise, KBF was able to go beyond supporting projects and carrying out public awareness to develop a third activity – promoting the content and structure of heritage protection.

The structural development of the sector included, for example in Flanders, the formation of four independent associations that have blossomed, fed by KBF's initial seed money and support. The Flanders Monument Watch, The Flemish Centre for Craft and Restoration, The Flemish Contact Commission for Heritage Protection and The Flemish Heritage Foundation exist today with the assistance of both public and private funding.

In 1998, KBF's heritage projects were integrated into the wider field of culture and sport, as a lever for social change and individual development. This fits in with the wider definition of concept of heritage used by KBF – movable and immovable; tangible and intangible. It represented a step away from the monuments sector, due to a change in roles and the independence acquired by the four associations. It also marked a change in direction: the foundation's research and actions called for an intersectoral, multidisciplinary approach that makes it possible to position heritage in society more effectively in, for example, neighbourhood and area development projects.

The Architectural Heritage Fund

Public enthusiasm grew to such an extent that from 1987, just five years into the programme, it was pushed to move forward in a number of other areas, including the issue of tax deductible gifts. Belgian legislation does not favour this tax treatment. As a result, there was no instrument available to those wishing to make donations to the heritage sector and receive a deduction. Because the foundation has a mandate to accept tax deductible gifts, it was decided to open "project accounts".

Through such accounts, individuals and corporations were able to support a specific heritage project, such as the restoration of an old field chapel or the conversion of a seventeenth-century building into a shelter for the homeless. Funds were sent to the foundation, which sent the contribution through to the project without taking any fees. The donor was then able to receive a tax deduction. This mechanism of facilitating gifts was – and is today – a huge success. Between 1987 and 2004 almost 300 projects were funded for more than €13 million.

By setting up such project accounts and managing the tax treatment of gifts, the foundation was able to find another avenue through which citizens could mobilise around the heritage cause.

Open Monuments Day

Launched in 1989, this event, held in the month of September, is still one of Belgium's most popular. The first day attracted hundreds of thousands of heritage lovers, and their numbers continue to rise. In 1992, the event took place in three regions and attracted more than 800 000 visitors. Today, it is managed by The Flanders Steering Group, which was managed by KBF. Open Monuments Day continues with more than 1 million visitors in 2004.

Lessons learned

The Architectural Heritage Programme ended in 1998, but its legacy lives on as the various initiatives and associations are continuing their work with the support of public funding. KBF has stepped back from the traditional monuments and countryside sector. The decoupling of the foundation's complementarity role with government and the public sector has not been without its challenges.

When KBF launched the heritage programme it commenced with very high ambitions, from raising awareness towards political change. That is, it wanted public authorities to take more responsibility (including financial support) for the heritage challenge facing Belgium. It was clear from the outset that to achieve this goal there was a need to work on different leverage points of change. One was to convince citizens and decision-makers visually through concrete renovations and new destinations for historical buildings. This was done over the years through grant-giving programmes for specific projects. Foundation grants were not the only financial resources; private donations and public money were also generated.

Extensive research continued throughout the programme, which provided the necessary facts and figures to make the case to decision-makers and contributed to the design of policies presented to politicians. This important policy work was complemented by an equally critical element of mobilisation, which was built into the programme through the Open Monument Days, organised by the foundation itself. The impressive and growing number of participants in these days convinced politicians that heritage was indeed important for the population and that the citizens (as voters) expected the public sector to take ownership of this issue.

To ensure that the sustainability of the foundation's innovative and creative role could be structurally embedded in the sector, it was essential to create a structure of active NGOs to ensure sustainability and long-term success. In the Belgian context the public authorities are critical players (both financially and for providing the legal framework); however, there was a strong conviction that civil society needed to have its voice heard – and listened to – to guarantee the dynamism needed for the future evolution of the sector.

This role was recognised in 2004 by the regional government of Flanders, which awarded one of KBF's programme officers a Prize for Cultural Heritage. The selection committee awarded the prize for the leverage instruments developed, the innovative approaches and efforts made to ensure the ongoing involvement of the various stakeholders in the sector – particularly citizens.

Selecting grants: working towards more accountability

Grants are a very important tactic, or building block, of a foundation's strategic methodology. Grants for third parties help to achieve a good balance between labour-intensive methods, such as conferences, reports and public education, and other capital-intensive methods. This ensures that salary costs do not become too high, thereby limiting budget flexibility. More importantly, grants are a way of recognising that actors in society, such as NGOs or academics, are supported for the work they do to achieve meaningful, sustainable change. This often involves activism and engaging in politics in a way that foundations generally cannot.

In many foundations, the selection of grants is prepared by programme officers for a board decision or decided upon by programme officers themselves. The selection and awarding of these grants is a key element of the accountability debate around foundations. The governance structure is also significant in this discussion. Nonetheless, the subject of grants and the process of grant-making is a highly sensitive issue on which foundations are criticised for being biased ideologically, or in some other way – particularly if selection is not done in a transparent, accountable manner or if it is made internally or by one person.

KBF has developed a methodology designed to increase its credibility and enhance its reputation. All the grants are decided upon by an independent selection committee, created around each specific field of programme activity or project. The selection committees are pluralistic. Their 10 members come from various ideological and philosophical backgrounds (without representing them) as well as from grassroots community organisations, NGOs, government, academia and the business community. In Belgium, the language balance is also taken into consideration by including French-, Flemish- and sometimes German-speaking members.

Each selection committee has a secretariat, comprising an external chair and a programme officer (who cannot vote), that prepares the follow up to the process. The KBF board delegates every aspect of grant selection to these committees, whose composition is approved by management. This working methodology has given KBF – a private foundation with a high profile public image – the reputation for impartiality and has surely contributed to its accountability and credibility.

Reaching towards innovation

This example clearly demonstrates that when one wants to achieve structural change – even in an area that is at first glance conservative because it is about conservation – one has to work creatively on different leverage points. This cannot be achieved through grants alone. The success achieved by deploying a spectrum of non-grant methodologies is not necessarily dependent upon creating long-term programmes. The tactics and methodologies used to tackle a global issue such as drug policy, discussed in Chapter 4, is another case in point.

It is evident from examples such as these – and the wealth of examples from across the sector – that effective philanthropy in the future must not be reduced to (albeit important) grant-giving activities alone. There is a diverse, rich range of methodologies available and it would be irresponsible not to use them, particularly if foundations plan to maintain a relevant position in today's complex societies.

Supporting children of imprisoned parents

KBF's project to support children of parents in prison is a good example of a shorter-term initiative that was sparked by foundation innovation, took root and grew, and is now supported by the public sector. The foundation supported the position of psychologists and others that children should continue to have contact with their parents, whatever a parent has done. It also believed that the circumstances in which children visited their parents in Belgian prisons were unacceptable, for both physical and psychological reasons.

The actors who possessed the leverage to achieve change were identified. First, the prisons are controlled and financed by the federal ministry of justice. Second, the psychological services that support prisoners' families are funded by Belgium's regional authorities. The foundation started by funding a research project that gave a clear overview of the problem. This research was published and presented during a seminar attended by all the interested parties. Next, KBF launched an advocacy initiative, beginning with meetings with the various responsible services. It proposed funding pilot projects on the condition that they would be followed by sustainable outcomes. This resulted in 12 prison projects where prisoners decorated rooms in a child-friendly way where they could meet with their children.

Material costs were covered by the federal budget. The foundation funded the psychological guidance and support in the first year, but regional governments assumed the funding in the second. In this way, KBF played a clear-cut catalysing and convenor role that reached well beyond pure grant-giving activities.

Living Heritage in southeast Europe

KBF's Living Heritage is a grant and capacity development programme aimed at supporting local community development in southeast Europe through the promotion of sustainable culture and heritage initiatives. The programme takes an innovative approach to heritage and its interaction with local communities. In this context, heritage is considered a valuable resource, a form of social capital that contributes to the environment and quality of life of local communities. The programme involves stakeholders in project development. Activities include:

- Working with local communities, public authorities, NGOs and other partners.
- Facilitating open, fair and participative processes in every stage of development of Living Heritage projects in order to establish mutual commitment and local ownership.
- Supporting appropriate sustainable heritage projects.
- Boosting local expertise, knowledge and organisational skills.
- Tailoring the work to the specificities of local situations.

The programme combines grant-making, capacity-building and technical assistance as well as evaluation and exchange of experience at local, national and regional level. It is carried out in partnership with financial partners and local coordinating organisations.

The programme is operating in Macedonia, Romania, Bulgaria, Bosnia and Herzegovina. During 1996–2000, several projects were supported in Latvia, Russia, the Czech Republic and Slovenia.

Venture philanthropy: a suitable model?

The suitability of the "new" venture approach to philanthropy is being questioned as a model. It is being held up – and hyped up – as the way forward by many in the USA and other countries characterised by the Anglo-Saxon model of civil society. It is also being encouraged by the growing number of "social entrepreneurs" funded by venture philanthropists who are emerging on both sides of the Atlantic.

The big plus of this "high engagement philanthropy" is the large number of new donors it has brought to the field, particularly those who profited in the new economy. Bringing this entrepreneurial spirit into the world of "old philanthropy" – the drive, the risk-taking, the innovation and the strong leadership – has been positive, as it is for the most part sorely lacking in the traditional philanthropic approach.

Lose–lose

However, behind this sexy concept some clear choices are to be made that bring with them equally clear downsides. A black-and-white view of the promises of venture philanthropy, put forward in *Board Member* magazine, outlines the debate:

> In an ideal vision of venture philanthropy, a funder provides a large sum of money to a non-profit, promises to continue funding it for years to come, and provides help with management skills, business training, financial and accounting systems, marketing strategy, technology and recruiting mentors – whatever the organisation needs to grow and prosper. A more grim view holds that the funder provides a cash infusion but then joins the board, clashing with long-time board members, meddling in management and threatening the organisation's very culture. The non-profit becomes dependent on the funder who then backs out leaving the non-profit high and dry.[13]

---

[13] "The promises of venture philanthropy", *Board Member*, Special Edition, May 2001, p. 13.

This is indeed a black-and-white view, but according to its many critics, venture philanthropy is a non-starter. Author Mark R. Kramer, who believes that foundations that behave as venture capitalists are engaging in a fantasy, describes the downsides very well. Kramer, a venture capital investment and strategy consultant, says it is "seriously misleading" because the tools of the venture capitalist will not work in philanthropy. "Applying a true venture-capital approach to grant-making would seriously distort the non-profit world, and merely bringing the terminology without the methodology will not allow foundations to achieve the success that venture capital has enjoyed," he warns.[14]

But the bad fit goes even deeper. In fact, it could be argued that the venture-capital approach to philanthropy undermines and restricts the various roles that foundations play within their societies, limiting them to that of service delivery or substitution. This is more understandable in the US in the face of a retreating state, where foundations and social entrepreneurs have a role to play in filling in the gaps. But venture philanthropists think more in terms of outcomes and deliverables than in terms of impact, which implies that they define performance in terms of a project or NGO they invest in rather than a complex societal problem to be addressed.

The complexity of any social problem – and its resolution – is never in the hands of one actor alone and the amount of money given by philanthropists is dwarfed by the public sector contributions of most governments. But even more importantly, the venture philanthropists' strong leadership and entrepreneurial spirit, which made them successful in the first place, is often coloured by a lack of modesty when it comes to "saving the planet". It is often a rude awakening when they discover that to achieve meaningful social and political change, other actors in civil society – and governments – control the levers. This causes inevitable tensions, which are aggravated by the fact that when

---

[14] Mark R. Kramer, "Venture capital and philanthropy: a bad fit", *The Chronicle of Philanthropy*, 22 April 1999, pp. 72–73.

working on root causes of society's ills, results are very difficult, sometimes impossible, to measure.

Win–win

There are several upsides to this approach to philanthropy. The infusion of the entrepreneurial spirit has been positive. It has given the somewhat sleepy sector a wake up call to become more aware than ever before of the need for accountability, bringing with it stricter evaluation and a need for more attention to the impacts of its actions and initiatives.

A venture philanthropist or social entrepreneur who ends up concentrating investments in NGOs and services to make them more efficient is likely to be driven by deliverables and measurable results, making them invaluable players in the non-profit sector. A way forward in the pluralistic world of philanthropy may be to encourage them to scale up their successful micro-solutions to address larger social problems requiring sustainable solutions to effect structural change and complement this work with advocacy and policy initiatives.

Venture philanthropy . . . European style

Venture philanthropy is a very Anglo-Saxon concept that hypes entrepreneurship and measurement. Its voluntarist language promotes the belief that individual leadership can change the world. It is no surprise that these ideas are just beginning to take root in continental Europe.

For example, the recently created European Venture Philanthropy Association at the moment primarily involves participants from the United Kingdom and the Netherlands. This initiative holds promise because it has the potential to reinforce the value of venture philanthropy across the continent. However, this model will not be presented as the one and only way forward for future philanthropists.

An interesting example of "European-style" venture philanthropy was born 10 years ago. La Fondation DEMETER, managed by La Fondation de France, assists and promotes charities and not-for-profit organisations, particularly those focusing on problems resulting from marginalisation and underdevelopment.

DEMETER's programmes are designed to optimise efficiency and management techniques. Its founders – European professionals working in finance, industry, consulting and the media – share an economic and social vision of perennial autonomy for the third sector. In particular, they strive to apply this vision to concrete projects. Operating members of DEMETER from France, the UK and Belgium are informed by an advisory board comprising experienced professionals in sectors where the foundation is active.

As an adviser, DEMETER provides free advice on achieving financial and operational efficiencies, fund-raising, and management techniques, as well as monitoring and control systems. As an investor, it develops or supports programmes active in social venture capital through micro-finance activities in emerging countries, such as India and Argentina.

DEMETER has been successful through its step-by-step, low-key approach to venture philanthropy; this has carved out solid ground upon which to build future successes.

4

The impact-driven foundation

If philanthropy is understood to be driven by social and political change, why do so many well-intentioned and well-endowed foundations stay within the narrow confines of grant-making or remain purely operational? The foundations that become "hybrid" are often viewed as rudderless organisations that cannot choose which path to follow. In fact, a true hybrid foundation is impact driven, which is arguably the way of the future. If meaningful social and political change is to take place, foundations must think beyond alleviating problems by making modest – and often unquantifiable – "improvements" to society, and act strategically by using the full range of methodologies available to them.

Today, given their privileged position, society expects much more of foundations – and rightly so. The US debate over the payout rate, and calls for more transparency and governance, are challenging the very legitimacy of foundations. A foundation's drive to create value must be validated by identifiable impact, otherwise it risks becoming part of the problem instead of part of the solution within the societies it serves. This dynamic does not yet necessarily hold true in Europe. However, it is very likely that just one scandal would open a Pandora's box of accountability.

The model of the impact-driven foundation is emerging, as foundations are increasingly using a strategic mix of grants, think tanks, advocacy, lobbying, citizen mobilisation and communication to achieve change that is defined by predetermined objectives. (The methodologies may change as the strategy unfolds, but the objectives usually remain fixed.) To be effective, foundations must identify – and exercise – the leverage points of change, one of which is to move off their traditionally neutral territory into a space where they can engage in a frank dialogue with their stakeholders, including donors, posing often tough questions and challenging the status quo.

Clearly, such engagement and advocacy has paid off for some of the more conservative foundations and institutions in the USA that have succeeded in shaping the public debate around issues such as education, health care and tax cuts. Foundations have a responsibility to engage in such public debates.

This type of engagement is out of character for many and it can be a risky business, particularly when dealing with politically charged social issues such as health care, the environment or immigration policy. However, foundations must take such risks, or risk coming under fire or, worse, becoming irrelevant.

Impact driven foundations deploy a wide range of methodologies to realise their objectives (Figure 4.1). A strategic mix of these tools is critical if they are to succeed.

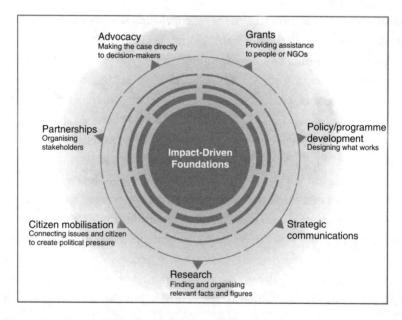

Figure 4.1   Impact-driven foundations*

* Graphic inspired by Frank Sharry, National Immigration Forum, USA.

Strategic philanthropy

Strategic philanthropy is different in different political and cultural surroundings. It is more reflective of society's needs and capacities, and because it is informed by stakeholder dialogue and engagement it can adapt to changing realities. In moving from reactive (or responsive) to proactive, foundations can become active in their communities and beyond by creating a platform for informed debate and setting an agenda for change.

Valuable lessons can be learned from the work of foundations outside the cultural and legal boundaries of the US and western Europe. Helmut Anheier and David Winder[1] write that many offer innovative potential as they develop more varied and proactive approaches to implementing their missions. Through a series of case studies, they have identified some of the more innovative practices, including:

- Working with other groups and sectors to catalyse change.
- Supporting the strengthening of civil society organisations.
- Social marketing.
- Testing and disseminating new approaches to social development.
- Maximising the impact of small grants programmes.
- Strategic planning to inform practice.

They write:

> A clear trend that emerges . . . is that foundations tend to move along a continuum from reactive to proactive. This appears to coincide with an evolution from responses that are motivated by charitable impulses to ones that look to address the underlying reasons for poverty.

Because many of these foundations are operating with modest resources, they seek to use them more strategically and seek out partnerships with civil society and governments at all levels. They are

---

[1] Helmut Anheier and David Winder, *Innovations in Strategic Philanthropy – comparative lessons from Africa, Asia, Central and Eastern Europe and Latin America*. Working paper for the International Network on Strategic Philanthropy. Gütersloh, Bertelsmann Foundation, 2004.

increasingly viewed as important players by local and national governments that recognise the value of the synergies that can be achieved through working in multi-stakeholder partnerships.

A new paradigm?

Complex challenges almost always involve a wide range of different actors who can play an invaluable role in solving them. Through stakeholder engagement and partnerships, it is possible to identify what is needed to effect the change necessary to address the underlying issues.

This is a rather new paradigm in today's world of philanthropy, but one that will go far to reaffirm the legitimacy of foundations as valuable players in their societies. As Matthew Miller points out: "Support a clinic for the uninsured, and you've done a wonderful thing. Change the debate about government's role in assuring basic health coverage for everyone, and you've solved the underlying problem."[2]

A good example of strategic, impact-driven philanthropy is the work initiated by Swiss philanthropist Stephan Schmidheiny, which is creating a dynamic around a political message. The political message is that the war on drugs is failing. His first step was to create a project through The Network of European Foundations for Innovative Cooperation (NEF), which became The European Drug Policy Fund. After an attempt to identify NGOs that qualified for capacity-building to enable them to engage strategically in the issue, the project launched its own media and advocacy organisation, with the aim of prodding European leaders into action to face the global drug war crisis.

The Senlis Council,[3] established in May 2002, serves as an international collaborative framework, which gathers expertise and facilitates new initiatives on global drug policy. The Council convenes politicians, high-profile academics, independent experts and NGOs. It is working

---

[2] Matthew Miller, "A challenge for liberal foundations", *The Chronicle of Philanthropy*, September 2003.
[3] http://www.senliscouncil.net

towards establishing itself as a dialogue partner with senior policy-makers at national and intergovernmental levels by fostering high-level exchanges and new ideas on integrated drug policies.

In September 2002, NEF established a Comité des Sages of European leaders, which reviewed the current state of drug policy at its meeting at the Foundation Oriente in Arrabida, Portugal. In March 2003, it released its Arrabida Conclusions at a press briefing in Brussels. Proposals for new international policy were set out in a document, *Global Drug Policy: Building a New Framework*, launched in February 2004, at a high-level meeting in Brussels during which the President of the European Parliament presented The Europe Prize in Excellence in Reporting on Global Drug Issues. The meeting was attended by European, international and national policy-makers and politicians.

The goal of implementing a pragmatic and effective drug policy discussion and moving beyond emotional and simplistic arguments is being realised: policy-makers, politicians and journalists are engaged. This is realising the goal of a living philanthropist who has become convinced that a certain issue, in this case, the global drug war, needed urgent attention. He wanted to begin to solve the problem now. He hired a political activist, created a relationship with a critical stakeholder (NEF), initiated a media and advocacy instrument (The Senlis Council) and launched research, meetings, events, media relations, advocacy and lobbying.

An overarching goal is to change the rigid UN drug policy defined under the UN's International Drug Control Programme, managed out of Vienna by the United Nations Office for Drug Control and Crime Prevention (UNODC). The foundation's convenor role in this initiative is not to specify how the treaty should be changed, but rather to ensure that the UNODC takes into account the experiences of different countries and integrates it into the global framework. This initiative is now part of the European Mercator Fund Project.

In this example, a philanthropist and the foundation sector are actively engaged in advocacy work around an urgent global issue to fill a capacity vacuum. It also brings together international agencies that do not always engage in dialogue and, as a result, often promote contradictory policies. Objectives are assessed quarterly and to date the project has exceeded its expectations of success.

This is an example of how the European foundation sector can show global leadership and become a strong player in shaping a new global policy. It reinforces the concept that foundations have a huge potential, far beyond their financial resources, particularly with their independence and privileged position.

An operational platform for collaboration

The Network of European Foundations for Innovative Cooperation (NEF)[4] is a compact and flexible organisation comprising 10 European-based foundations. Until January 2002, the organisation was known as the Association of Innovative Cooperation in Europe. NEF serves as a platform for launching cooperative projects at European level. NEF is filling a niche, with a scope to form a stronger process of partnership, building on issues of priority concern where foundations voluntarily recognise the added value of mounting initiatives together. Such cooperation is breaking new ground in Europe and is attracting the interest of other foundations, as well as that of EU institutions.

Its members work around clusters of priority issues/themes for the network to address. NEF has initiated several programmes in the areas of youth empowerment, citizen's fundamental rights, education and culture, and global governance (under which falls the European Drug Policy Fund).

For example, NEF funded the Free Movement Solidarity Fund, a project that ran from 1999 to 2003. Supported by the Charities Aid Foundation and the King Baudouin Foundation and managed by the European Citizen Action Service (ECAS), the fund provides legal assistance to individuals encountering problems in exercising their economic, social and political rights under European Union law or obtaining redress across borders. NEF funding gave ECAS the added advantage of being independent from the EU institutions, which enabled it to pursue individual cases in more depth.

---

[4] http://www.nef-web.org/

Many of the cases are referred by European Members of Parliament. Areas of concern include travelling and staying in another country, whether as worker, job-seeker or pensioner; recognition of qualifications, health care and social security coordination; and cross-border consumer transactions. The fund provides legal information and, when necessary, actively helps and provides financial aid for people confronted with obstacles in the exercise of their rights. Today, ECAS has integrated the fund – and fund-raising – into its portfolio of activities and the advocacy work continues. It is now financed by the EU.

Identifying the leverage points of change

There are different leverage points of change depending on the issue, the time and the context, as well as the level of sophistication of a society and its civil society model. Similarly, there are different paradigms about the actions or levers that effect change. Historically, the liberal US foundations, such as Carnegie and Rockefeller, and in Europe, the Volkskwagen Foundation (Germany) and Stiftlesen Riksbankens Jubileumsfond (Sweden), have relied on research activities, which Miller describes as "social science" in that the main way they shape social change is by supporting research. "Experts study problems, discern the answers, publish them, and enlightened policymakers put the fixes in place," he writes. He also points out that such a grant-making strategy cannot suffice to move public debate in today's political and media culture.[5]

Today, there appears to be some agreement in the foundation world on the paradigm that change is achieved through funding civil society groups. The danger of working within just one paradigm (such as through research and civil society funding) is that often, to address complex

[5] Ibid.

social problems, there is a need to play on different leverage points of change. This reinforces the argument that to be effective, foundations must think in terms of "and–and" instead of "or–or".

The same applies to foundations that act purely as grant-makers. They literally "grant" themselves into a box where often they become ineffective because they no longer understand the constantly changing environment in which they operate. In this way, they smother themselves by rendering their well-intentioned philanthropy almost meaningless. Band-aid solutions do not work in complex societies. In fact, grants can often exacerbate an already deteriorating situation by failing to empower those civil society organisations that lack the capacity to sustain long-term social and/or political change.

Timothy E. Wirth, President of the United Nations Foundation and Better World Fund, in a paper delivered in June 2003, points out that these early years of the twenty-first century look a lot different from the heyday of philanthropy, as it has traditionally been known, when it had a point of view, new ideas, bold initiatives and even influence within governments at all levels. Ideas became realities back then because progressive philanthropies sponsored careful research, developed applied policy to reflect the research findings, trained a cadre to carry out the policy within generously supported institutions, explained their policies to the public, and had a receptive ear in government.

He believes this agenda has been taken up by today's more conservative foundations that have been, and are still, advocating for welfare reform, school vouchers, medical savings accounts and the mainstreaming of faith-based institutions. The changes unfolding in US society are being built through:

> The careful and focused use of the levers of democratic government: the generation of ideas, transforming them into policy, marketing of the policy changes, the cultivation of public leadership, the persuasion (lobbying) of policy-makers and the building of a constituency base.[6]

---

[6] Timothy E. Wirth, *The Need for Philanthropic Advocacy*. Remarks at the Global Philanthropy Forum Conference on Borderless Giving, Stanford, California, June 2003.

One of the most important leverage points of change is public opinion. Politicians are forced for the sake of their survival to respond to the voting public. If a foundation can connect issues and citizens to exert political pressure, it has in its hands a powerful force to create change. Citizen mobilisation and strategic communications, including media relations, are critical to this process.

Stakeholder engagement is critical

Some critics observe that a foundation's interaction with stakeholders could be a mere public relations exercise to build more public trust and avoid excessive regulation. This is myopic. However, others question the difference between foundations dispensing grants to advocacy groups and doing the work themselves – and rightly so. The public should question the right of foundations to embark into advocacy work, as foundations are not endowed with democratic legitimacy. For these reasons, stakeholder engagement is essential to the issues of credibility and legitimacy. Such engagement gives foundations the backing to respond to those who ask the accountability question: "Whom do you represent?"

Such engagement is fundamental if one is to identify the leverage points of change and become as effective as possible. It is also a foundation's obligation, as it can provide a neutral platform for informed debate. A foundation can choose any bottom line it wishes. As such, it has a responsibility to exercise this freedom in a way that serves the public interest. In effect, involving stakeholders turns principle into practice by involving the communities that foundations wish to serve.

Ruth Tebbets Brousseau, in her interview with (US) Council on Foundations' Scrivner Award recipient Mary Mountcastle, Trustee of the A. Smith Reynolds Foundation, reports that one of the pillars of creativity in creative grant-making is "crossing boundaries and mixing worlds".

She quotes Mountcastle:

(The) creative process for foundations is thinking very intentionally about how you bring people together who cross all the fault lines of race and class; public, private and non-profit perspectives; grounds that include grassroots voices, a policy point of view and other kind of technical expertise. There's a real magic in all those people coming together, learning from each other, and trying to move towards ways that they can all work together.[7]

The synergy emanating from foundations' extraordinary convening power can spark new partnerships, galvanise political agendas and ignite political and social change.

Because of the complexity of the Belgian national framework – three official languages, coalition governments and a very weak foundation culture (there was no legal framework until April 2003) – the King Baudouin Foundation has positioned itself as a impact-driven foundation, which means that stakeholder interaction is critical to its functioning as an effective agent of change. Key stakeholder groups are represented on the Board of Directors. All the grants are decided upon by independent, 10-member, pluralistic selection committees, including people from community organisations, NGOs, governments, academia and the business community. Advisory committees give input into think tanks and KBF's advocacy work. Stakeholders also participate in the foundation's strategic planning, which is reviewed every three or four years through surveys, hearings and in-depth interviews.

In their survey of effective foundations in emerging economies, Anheier and Winder note that, in the context of strategic planning, research is complemented or replaced by convening key groups around the issue at hand and collectively identifying next steps in terms of the most appropriate role for the foundation to play. This is a "very deliberate attempt by the foundation to listen to its stakeholders and secure ideas and buy in from these stakeholders

---

[7] Ruth Tebbets Brousseau, *Experienced Grantmakers at Work, When Creativity Comes Into Play*, The Foundation Center, January 2004, p. 38.

on the foundation's role and the issues it should address".[8] In other words, it was central to developing the foundation's strategic focus.

Keeping an ear to the ground

Stakeholder engagement is a serious business within the King Baudouin Foundation's social justice programme under which a Listening Network has been set up. One of the objectives of the programme is to publicise new forms of social injustice or forgotten forms of social injustice, with a view to laying the groundwork for a workable solution.

Because the governments through various institutional levels are taking care of most of the social problems in Belgium, the value-added role of a foundation is to be quicker off the mark by becoming closer to the people to discover the manifestations of social injustice in all its forms. To this end, KBF identified more than 250 individuals from different backgrounds whose mission is to provide a written report in the form of stories concerning the social injustices they discover in their working and living environments.

The Listening Network includes social and educational workers and representatives from the NGO sector. Perhaps more importantly, KBF has recruited people from all walks of life, including police officers, shop owners, pharmacists, butchers, newsagents and hairdressers. Also involved are journalists, trades union representatives and religious leaders.

Members of the network are asked to feed the foundation with stories of injustice, but for those who are uncomfortable with the

---

[8] Ibid.

writing process, young journalists conduct an interview and compile a
report. In 2003, 240 stories were registered and clustered around 65
themes, which were discussed by a Decoding Committee. The committee then decided which themes would be tackled through KBF's
various programmes and projects through grant-giving, research
studies, seminars, advocacy or a combination of methodologies.

This form of stakeholder involvement is clearly an experiment, but it
is showing promise. Fourteen projects have emerged from this work,
covering a wide range of issues, including young runaways, the plight of
foreign domestic workers, the status and treatment of foreigners in
Belgian prisons, and the particular problems faced by the elderly.
(In Belgium, the majority of the population older than 80 years are
women, facing issues such as isolation and mobility.)

Forging strategic partnerships

A natural progression from stakeholder engagement is striking up
mutually beneficial multi-stakeholder partnerships. Forging such
strategic alliances is almost a prerequisite to effecting social and
political change. Anheier and Winder recognised this dynamic in
their study of foundations in emerging economies – because of
limited resources, they could not tackle very complex and dynamic
problems. They recognised the strength that comes from working in
consort with other sectors, as well as by supporting change on complementary levels. In some cases, strategic alliances ensured a higher
quality of response to social concerns. In all cases, they are likely to
build on and nurture the foundation's chosen niche or comparative
advantage.[9]

The work on drug policy is a testament to the power of multi-
stakeholder partnerships and strategic alliances. The King Baudouin

---

[9] Ibid.

Foundation's heritage initiative (see Chapter 3) depended on partnership with key community players. Effective partnerships last as long as necessary to achieve the objectives. They optimise existing resources and bring new ones into play. In addition, they can ramp up existing advocacy work at community, national or international level.

Many forms of partnership are developing between business, government, trades unions and other civil society organisations. The fine line between business and the rest of the world is blurring, and the private sector is rapidly becoming a fully engaged partner in civil society. Such partnerships represent an important source of innovation in both practical action at local level and policy-making at national and international levels. In part, these new social partnerships are forming because of the immense changes being created by the emerging architecture of the global economy and the trickle-down effects to local and regional level.

Building a platform for strategic philanthropy is no easy task, but the changing nature of strategic partnerships represents a window of opportunity for foundations – by taking advantage of their unique position in society, they could become the important catalysts of change they aspire to be.

Not without difficulties...

An important element in the trade-off involved in engaging in partnerships is the levels of control one actor can exercise upon a societal problem. Clearly, on many issues foundations are just one player – and a small one at that. At the same time, they have the advantage of being a credible player with resources (money, expertise, providing a neutral forum, and the luxury of taking a long-term perspective if necessary) that place them in a unique position to create value.

Rare are the structural problems that a foundation can solve alone – there are almost always different actors involved who can work towards a solution. In this respect, if a foundation is truly to exercise its role of social or political change or as a convenor, it is almost forced into partnerships with other players. NGOs, media, government agencies, research institutes and sometimes advocacy groups are necessary partners in the search for creating public benefit by innovative problem-solving.

These strategic partnerships often redefine the classic power relationship that exists between grant-giver and grantee. For example, within a partnership with an NGO, the foundation contributes more than funds and the NGO gives invaluable input to the project, as in the Sustainable Food Laboratory initiative. The traditional grantee-grant-giver relationship then becomes a strategic partnership.

The difficulty of partnerships in the foundation world is at least two-fold. First, foundations are by nature individualistic creatures. They have money, which often gives them the illusion of holding the truth—a particularly unhelpful attitude to bring into a meaningful partnership. Partnerships require openness to the agenda and the cultures of others, as well as compromises and the sharing of eventual successes.

A second difficulty lies in the inherent differences of the philanthropic impulse. If the impulse comes from a business person who, over the years, has had the experience of moving the market using his or her own energy, ideas and determination, it is often a difficult step for that person to understand that complex societal problems cannot be resolved solely by individuals. Such problems are usually solved within partnerships with colleagues (thereby requiring greater scale), or with other stakeholders (achieving greater impact).

Achieving ambitious changes together

The Sustainable Food Laboratory, a project seed-funded by the W.K. Kellogg Foundation, The Charles Leopold Mayer Foundation and the King Baudouin Foundation, is a good example of a horizontal initiative executed by a structured, strategic multistakeholder, multi-continent partnership. The objective is to create food supply chains that are economically, environmentally and socially sustainable – being at once profitable and affordable, in balance with nature, and good for producer and consumer communities.

The project brings together leaders from business, governments, farm groups and NGOs in dialogue and action to achieve changes that are more ambitious than they could achieve separately, with a view to moving food produced in a sustainable manner from niche to mainstream.

Deliverables include creating five to 10 prototypes and pilots of mainstream sustainable food supply chains. The Lab Team includes production, processing, marketing and consumer leaders on three continents. Living, functioning models to sustain food supply chains will be created. The prototypes will be of systems that can grow to be dynamic, mainstream, enduring and profitable at each stage.

This will be accomplished by bringing together a diverse team of 35 entrepreneurial leaders to create what many of them have already learned they cannot create alone: innovative, cross-boundary supply chains, attractive to investment, harmonious with environmental resources, and appealing to customers. The team members, primarily from Europe, the US and Brazil, represent a microcosm of the stake-holders in these supply chains, including farmers, farm workers, processors, wholesalers, retailers, consumers, representatives of government agencies, activist, financiers and researchers.

The Lab Team is supported by a group of Executive Champions, high-level representatives, including CEOs of the companies and organisations with which team members are affiliated. The Champions provide feedback and credibility, as well as support for mobilising further resources as laboratory projects take shape.

This is an ambitious project, but already, the partnership is delivering results.

Recognising innovative philanthropy

The first annual Raymond Georis Prize for Innovative Philanthropy in Europe was awarded at the European Foundation Centre's 15th Annual General Assembly and Conference, June 2004. Avila Kilmurray, the Executive Director of The Community Foundation for Northern Ireland, was recognised for her contribution to European peace and security through its peace-building and social solidarity work both in Ireland and in the Balkans.

The award, an initiative of the European Mercator Fund, emphasises the important role that European foundations and the European philanthropic community play in the future of peace and security in Europe through innovative projects.

"It was our role to be accessible, flexible and a listening organisation for activists," said Kilmurray. "We played a critical role of having a finger on the pulse of developments and an ear to the ground. The limited resources we have can play a critical part in changing circumstances by being targeted and timely."

She emphasised that innovation is not about what is novel, but about more adventurous ways of doing things and having a keen eye to the niche opportunity for social change and progress: "Innovation is also about risk-taking and analysing the outcomes of such ventures. It is not always about money, but also about vision, people and flexibility."

By giving small, well-targeted grants, as well as providing policy and development support, the foundation demonstrates the essential role that foundations play both in their local communities and on a pan-European level. The Community Foundation for Northern Ireland works with both the Protestant and the Catholic Communities. In addition, it plays a significant role in the administration of the EU Programmes for Peace and Reconciliation in Northern Ireland and the Border Region of Ireland, which addresses the economic and social issues needed to support Northern Ireland's transition to a more peaceful and stable society. This is an anomaly as the European Commission rarely, if ever, works with foundations as an intermediary for funding.

The foundation has initiated five operational YouthBanks in Serbia, Bosnia and Croatia. These were based on the experience from Northern Ireland of the operation involving Catholic and Protestant young people working together to identify need, promote philanthropy and take decisions to assist local youth activity.

The YouthBank project revolves around community relations, the exploration of identity, and the development of understanding, trust and respect, as well as issues around conflict resolution. The foundation offers a model for efforts in other divided communities with its considerable record of achievement in building peace in Northern Ireland and has exported the project to other regions ravaged by conflict.

(Created by philanthropist Stephan Schmidheiny in 2003, the European Mercator Fund's[10] objective is to deal with matters related to Europe's role in global social issues. As an initiative inside the Network of European Foundations, it hopes to act as a catalyst for programmes or initiatives in areas where European foundations could form partnerships with each other and in cooperation with others around the world on pressing global issues.)

Advocacy: standing up for political and social change

As direct service delivery will almost never effect a long-term change, foundations are being urged to become more vocal, direct actors in their communities. Miller says that today's leverage is in ideas. He calls upon foundations to cooperate in new ways and to emphasise macro questions of taxation and spending in ways that have not traditionally been their focus. He argues that "timidity" over legal limits on foundation-supported advocacy has produced a vacuum among foundations that should be free to lead. Miller also points out that conservative US foundations have managed to move the national debate to the right while operating within the existing legal framework.

[10] http://www.mercatorfund.org

Shaping the public debate around controversial issues (such as health care and education in the US and drug policy and the migration issue in Europe) is a critical role for foundations. Yet most are uncomfortable with the notion of advocacy or lobbying and fall back on their role of being a neutral player. Arguably, this type of *laissez-faire* attitude preserves the status quo, which is precisely what impact-driven foundations are trying to change.

Wirth implores foundations to engage in greater philanthropic advocacy:

> You have a point of view, and you need policy allies to help argue before the public. Engage the media, walk the legislative corridors, and persuade government officials. If you don't join the policy debate, you have an absolute chance of not winning it.

Wirth urges foundations that want to make a better world to make more use of governmental institutions:

> If we believe in what we are funding, and are hopeful about replicability, we have to work the system. This means that we have to educate, persuade and sometimes lobby our government. Good laws and good governance are essential to good public policy and I for one want to help define what "good" means.

Risk-averse behaviour does not advance strategic philanthropy nor does it befit the impact-driven foundation. When considering a project or initiative, it is essential to assess the situation, set objectives, identify the levers of change and devise a strategy to get there. This involves solid risk management assessment, but it must be carefully balanced with the benefits of taking risks and daring to win. These risks include involving stakeholders and donors in an honest dialogue about what effecting change involves – and how far the foundation's supporters are willing to go to achieve it.

Alliance magazine poses the question: "For a field that talks about results, what could be more important than assuming the political and financial risks necessary to achieve those results?" The article goes on to challenge:

> Too often, philanthropic institutions don't get past their gauzy visions of making the world a better place. In refusing to take a position on tough policy debates,

they betray the claim that they are delivering results, solving tough problems, and taking on the big challenges.[11]

A conundrum exists in that the outcome of advocacy and lobbying activities are often difficult – if not impossible – to measure, but their return on investment (of time, money and energy) over the long term is just as often invaluable.

The advocacy dilemma

A classic reaction to the concept of foundations adding advocacy work to their toolbox of methodologies is: "You cannot do that; who do you represent?" This is a perfectly valid question, which reinforces the need for foundations to practise meaningful stakeholder engagement and to work in partnership. By involving stakeholders in developing "the case" being advocated under the foundation's leadership, the question is answered.

A very accountable way of working, one would think.

The puzzling aspect about advocacy and the work of foundations is that many eschew this activity, claiming that they cannot operationalise and carry out advocacy themselves, primarily as it may be perceived as being too political. But what is the difference between working backed by the legitimacy of stakeholder engagement and the direct funding of civil society or NGOs to carry out the advocacy work?

This is both troubling and, arguably, hypocritical as the foundation maintains its distance from a potentially politically sensitive issue, yet funds others to deal with it. Many foundations hide behind this form of subcontracting, allowing the technical difference to mask their activities. Governments, stakeholders and donors can surely see through this, which perversely could damage a foundation's credibility.

---

[11] "What is social justice philanthropy?" *Alliance*, Volume 8, Number 3, September 2003, p. 37.

There are legitimate reasons why foundations choose to fund others to carry out projects – it is important that they strike the right methodological balance between operational and grant-giving activities that suit their programming objectives. But this should not prevent direct advocacy work if the situation demands this type of activity.

Ford under fire

The Ford Foundation came under fire in the wake of the protests that disrupted the UN World Conference Against Racism in Durban, South Africa in August 2001. Thousands of human rights activists from around the globe attended the conference, which was disrupted – and many claim derailed – by anti-Jewish hecklers.

The Ford Foundation, which granted $35 million to Arab and pro-Palestinian organisations in 2000 and 2001, was labelled a "major Palestinian activist funder" by NGOs and others monitoring the protests. These groups made different statements that upset some prominent Jewish organisations, which asked the Ford Foundation to explain the motivation behind these grants.

In 2003, following a letter of inquiry from a US congressman asking whether Ford had funded NGOs engaged in incitement of anti-Semitism at Durban, the foundation added a clause to its standard grant letter of agreement. The language includes this clause: "By countersigning this grant letter, you agree that your organization will not promote or engage in violence, terrorism, bigotry or the destruction of any state, nor will it make sub-grants to any entity that engages in these activities."

This unfortunate situation further illustrates the advocacy dilemma and reinforces the argument: there is really no difference between a foundation engaging in advocacy work itself or funding others to do it. Under both options the foundation is open to criticism.

This is not a plea to cease giving advocacy grants. It simply reiterates that funding advocacy is not a sufficient argument against those who challenge the right of foundations to advocate for change.

Communication is essential

Foundations in general do not do a good job of communicating their objectives. The foundation world informs itself through countless publications, websites, conferences, seminars and associations, but few reach beyond this tight circle of colleagues. The impact-driven foundation will not succeed if it doesn't communicate what it is trying to accomplish, for how else can it engage in meaningful stakeholder dialogue, mobilise citizens and change public opinion? For this is essential to a change strategy.

A report by the Williams Group, funded by The David and Lucile Packard Foundation Knowledge Project, points out that foundations are also poor communicators among themselves. The report urges that foundations step beyond the typical dissemination approach and start thinking in terms of from R&D to market: "Some obstacles come from the structure, incentives and culture of philanthropy. Others come from a tradition of poor communications practice by the sector's purveyors of knowledge, whether foundations or non-profit groups."[12]

Arguably, these obstacles also thwart external communication efforts. The Williams Group offers three techniques to produce content with impact: clear messages, provocative arguments and memorable stories. Foundations are good at producing memorable stories, but most often fail at the first two. There are, of course, exceptions, including the global drug policy initiative driven by The Mercator Fund.

In February 2004, the Interest Group on Migration of the European Foundation Centre convened a stakeholder seminar, *Closing the Communications Gap – strategies for a dialogue between migration stakeholders and the media*. Concerned about hostile public opinion towards migrants, seminar participants wanted to learn how to turn the situation around. At the table was Frank Sharry of the National Immigration Forum, US, who has been working on communication issues surrounding migration for a number of years.

---

[12] Williams Group, *Marketing Your Knowledge: A Report to Philanthropies R&D Organizations*, The David and Lucile Packard Foundation Knowledge Project, 2004.

Representatives from the media explained challenges they face in getting information and meeting deadlines. Sharry told participants that on the issue of migrants and immigration, strategic communications is at the heart of creating change. He acknowledged that the communications challenge regarding this issue is "formidable" but warned that even if pragmatic, strategic communications must be principled, not manipulative. This involves speaking up to the right people, knowing your audience, developing powerful messages and recruiting compelling messengers. The National Immigration Forum hired a political marketing research firm to test their messages, only to discover that for each person they might convince, they were setting three against them.

According to Sharry, public opinion can be measured through a "10–40–40–10%" formula, whereby 10% of the public are negative towards and issue and 10% are positive; the 80% in the "soft middle" can be swayed either way. In effect, communications aiming at the 10% on each end of the spectrum are wasted. Foundations often make the mistake of preaching to the converted. Unless the message reaches the soft middle, the chance of moving public opinion is greatly reduced. The potential influence of communication is immeasurable; it is one of a foundation's most valuable resources, and this power tool must be handled with skill and precision.

Developing a powerful message that resonates with the public is essential, but this message must also be backed by stories that put a human face on the issue. Again, working in partnership with partners that Sharry refers to as "unusual allies" is often a powerful multiplier. A report on a Rockefeller Foundation Bellagio Conference notes:

> For positive social change to advance and lives around the world to improve, communications, as a discipline, must be better integrated into social change theories. Its power to move individuals, cultures, institutions and nations is essential on the continuum of change.[13]

---

[13] *Communications and Social Change: Forging Strategies for the 21st Century*. A report on a Rockefeller Foundation Bellagio Conference, April 1997.
http://www.rockfound.org/Documents250/cands.html

Communicating for social change is a process that is taking place in a rapidly changing environment in which different methodologies are required. Citizens, particularly those with Internet access, often find themselves drowning in a sea of data and information. An effective communications strategy must penetrate this "noise" using a mix of vehicles including speeches, debates, written materials, newspaper quotes, radio and television appearance, press conferences, rallies, fund-raising pitches and meetings with policy-makers and opinion leaders. It must also make use of traditional and information age communication technologies in a horizontal approach, rather than a top-down hierarchical model.

Funding news media projects

Not only do foundations generally fail at communicating what they do, they do not take advantage of opportunities to fund news-media projects that could draw more public attention to their causes. As environment journalist Dale William[14] writes, US foundations spend billions of dollars on environmental efforts, but put very little into news-media projects that could raise awareness about critical issues. "If no one is able to hear of that good work, is it very effective?" he queries.

Journalists in mainstream media do not consistently cover the environmental issues that threaten our planet. Because Americans turn to broadcast media for the major portion of their news, broadcasting is particularly critical; it plays a significant role in determining the national agenda. William points out that less than 2% of all news coverage on US commercial network broadcasts involves environmental stories, and that journalists need specialised knowledge to cover complex environment issues. Foundations should be seriously

---

[14] Dale William, A low-cost way to help the environment, *The Chronicle of Philanthropy*, 10 June 2004, pp. 41–43.

considering the area of journalism training. In addition, public broad-casts that focus on environmental issues are rapidly disappearing through lack of funding.

William points to one "bright spot" in this otherwise bleak picture. The National Science Foundation recognises the need for more environ-mental reporting and is providing at least $6 million to public television shows and almost $1 million to radio for science reporting, including coverage of the environment. But these grants are the exception rather than the rule. He calls upon private foundations to step up and focus on the "urgent need for a stronger, more vibrant news media".

Engaging media

Working with the media can involve pure dissemination of foundation achievements and funded projects. If one focuses on the impact of each project, it appears evident that, in some cases, the media go beyond reporting what the foundation is doing to become an actor in its strategy or a partner in its work.

Involving the fourth estate as a stakeholder results in a positive spin-off in that journalists better understand the role of foundations in society. KBF's programme on the multicultural society involves trying to create a more positive public attitude towards migrant communities and more specifically to Muslim communities in Belgium and across Europe. In trying to create a better understanding and perception, the media is undoubtedly a valuable actor in creating change.

For this reason, a project was created that gives journalists from Belgium, Turkey and Morocco the opportunity to be immersed for a month in another country. For example, Belgian journalists travel to Turkey and Morocco where they write about the sociopolitical and cultural context of the country, with a special emphasis on the countries and regions where migrants in Belgium come from. Their reports are published in the Belgian press. Turkey and Moroccan journalists visit migrant communities in Belgium and report on the more general issues of Belgium and the European Community. Their work is disseminated in their home countries and in Belgium.

Effective media relations involves developing a relationship of trust with the fourth estate. Through such a partnership, foundations can help to overcome the so-called "if it bleeds, it leads" phenomenon that can be highly damaging if, and when, irregularities occur in the foundation world. A deeper understanding of the role of foundations and their potential for value creation is a win–win situation for both media and philanthropists.

Greater expectations...

A report released in April 2004 from The Center for Effective Philanthropy emphasises that non-profit leaders value foundations with approachable and responsive staff members, clearly spelled out goals, and demonstrated expertise in the fields in which they work. Less important is the size and type of grants they receive.

The report, *Listening to Grantees: What Nonprofits Value in their Foundation Funders*,[15] dispels many myths concerning the relationship between grantees and foundations. It also notes that grantees rated foundations positively in terms of overall satisfaction as well as perceptions of foundation impact. The report, the result of a survey of more than 9000 grantees, identifies three key dimensions that non-profit organisations most value in foundation funders:

- Quality of interactions with foundation staff: fairness, responsiveness, and approachability.
- Clarity of communications of a foundation's goals and strategy: clear and consistent articulation of objectives.

---

[15] http://www.effectivephilanthropy.com/publications/publications-overview.html

- Expertise and external orientation of the foundation: understanding of fields and communities of funding and ability to advance knowledge and affect public policy.

The lesson for foundations aiming to improve relations with charities is that they must make the necessary investments in administrative costs to meet each charity's needs. When releasing the report, Phil Buchanan, Executive Director of the Center, pointed out that people often equate administrative costs with waste.

"The survey shows that there are many things grantees value and many important roles that foundations play which require (them) to spend money beyond grant-making," he said. "As long as it is done responsibly, it will improve foundations' key relations with their non-profit partners and the impact they have."[16]

The conclusions of this report will inevitably surface in the US debate concerning payout rates and administrative costs. But the message coming through loud and clear from grantees should resonate with foundations in Europe and world wide: they are increasingly expecting foundations to play a stronger leadership role and more effectively deploy the wide-range of methodologies they have at their disposal. In addition, they are implicitly seeking proof of foundation impact.

---

[16] Debra Blum, "Grant seekers say they value foundation expertise", *The Chronicle of Philanthropy*, 29 April 2004, p. 11.

5

A payout rate for foundations: A roadmap for Europe

The panoply of foundations' roles is being debated and challenged regularly. As communities grapple with the unanticipated consequences of increasingly globalised market economies, the credibility and legitimacy of foundations are at stake. Their critics view them as a control mechanism for private wealth, whereby society's privileged families or corporations can "warehouse" large sums of tax-sheltered income, shrouded in secrecy and with a minimum of public accountability. Many say these "warehouses" should focus on developing more effective and efficient systems of inventory and distribution – that is, more strategic and accountable ways of operating.

Several observers view foundations as a convenient conduit for tax evasion and argue that this loss of tax revenues (which are in effect government expenditures) represents a substantial cost to society. This cost must be offset by initiating value-added services to society, thus contributing to the welfare of its citizens. In Chapter 1 of this book, Michael Porter and Mark Kramer report that foundations do not invest the majority of their assets to philanthropic causes. In fact, in the US, just 0.01% of foundation investment portfolios is invested to support philanthropic purposes.

Foundations are also busy creating financial returns because they have an obligation to their donors and trustees to invest assets to ensure perpetuity, which in turn raises the complex issue of intergenerational responsibility – the question of continuing family/corporate control versus a foundation's charitable activities. Does society have an obligation to subsidise future generations, arguably at the expense of today's citizens? Therein lies a tension that has been the subject of public debate for more than 50 years.

What are the policy consequences of today's favourable tax status of foundations? In the US, the debate has been heating up again for the first time since the enactment of the Tax Reform Act in 1969, which imposed a 6% (later revised to 5% in 1981) annual minimum distribution requirement. Popularly referred to as a payout rate, this figure refers to average endowment assets. Porter and Kramer note that, on average, US foundations distribute just 5.5% of their assets to charity each year, a number slightly above the legal minimum. In practice, the legal requirement has become the maximum amount distributed.

In Europe, there is no annual minimum distribution requirement. Helmut Anheier and Diana Leat maintain that in Britain very few foundations meet the 5% payout rate.[1] It is estimated that foundations in Europe have an actual payout rate around 4%. There is a danger in that if European foundations do not impose a form of voluntary payout rate upon themselves in a legitimate and accountable framework of self-regulation, national authorities or the European Council or the European Parliament may do it for them.

No clear picture in Europe

Because there is no legal requirement for a payout rate, known as a spending rate in Europe, it is very difficult to get a clear picture. Existing figures are incomplete and based on voluntary surveys that guarantee

---

[1] Helmut Anheier and Diana Leat, "From charity to creativity: philanthropic foundations in the 21st century", *Comedia*, 2002, p. 69.

anonymity. Figures from the European Foundation Financial Investment Officers (EFFIO) based on a survey of 13 foundations, including some of Europe's largest, report spending rates of between 3% and 5% for 2003 and an average of 3.34%. In 2002, the average was 4.78%.

A survey done for this book of the top 25 European foundations resulted in 14 returns and spending rates of 4.3% for 2003 and 4.8% for 2004. The lowest spending rate reported in 2004 was 2.4% and the highest 8%. This glimpse of the situation indicates that the average spending rate does not match the 5% payout rule in the US. In addition, there are important differences year to year and between foundations.

A legacy of controversy

In the US, critics abound, particularly in the wake of public scepticism. Pablo Eisenberg, writing in *The Chronicle of Philanthropy*, maintains that if the payout rate in the US were raised by just 1% to 6% in grants only, the result would add more than $7 billion annually to the collective income of non-profit organisations. He argues:

> Despite their enormous growth over the past 20 years, foundations are still required to distribute only 5% of their net assets each year – the minimal rate set by Congress in 1981. It is time for Congress to raise that figure. In exchange for their substantial tax benefits, foundations have an obligation to share a fair burden of the costs of maintaining a vibrant non-profit world and a healthy civil society. Unfortunately, foundations collectively have regarded the legal payout as a ceiling, not a floor.[2]

---

[2] Pablo Eisenberg, "Congress should increase amount foundations must give", *The Chronicle of Philanthropy*, 27 June 2002.

The payout debate is again escalating in the US for several reasons, including public scepticism in the wake of several scandals and because of the state's retreat from providing social services to its citizens. Eisenberg points to recent developments that have endangered the US's social welfare programmes and the financial situation of charities, including:

- Serious cutbacks in many federal social programmes.
- The recent recession.
- The loss of state revenue.
- Massive tax cuts for the wealthiest citizens.
- The growing inequality of wealth and income.
- Increases in homelessness.
- Decreases in low-cost housing.
- The growing competition for scarce funds among non-profit groups.

"For these reasons the expectations of and the demands on institutional philanthropy have grown. Whether grant-makers will respond with more resources will be a serious test of foundations' relevancy," he says. "Surely foundations can do much more. The growth in their assets has been phenomenal, far outpacing the increase in grants they have distributed to charities."

(This is true when one views such growth over the long-term, despite market losses in the years 2000 to 2002.)

This is the nexus of the debate occurring in the United States. It should serve as a wake-up call to European foundations that have been operating below the radar screen of national and European legislators in a (heretofore positive) policy vacuum. Eisenberg's arguments may not apply fully to the European context, as foundations are not solely about grant-giving to civil society, nor are they expected to fill the gap left by the state. However, what is happening in the US should serve as a bellwether for European foundations as they confront national legislative frameworks and a conceivably imposed Europe-wide framework.

The US experience

As early as 1950, there were rumblings in the US Congress regarding the favourable tax treatment of charitable foundations. These rumblings were grounded in distrust, expressed by President Harry Truman in his address to Congress and reiterated by his Treasury Secretary John W. Snyder, who explained the Administration's concerns: "Another...abuse of tax exemption involves the establishment of so-called charitable foundations or trusts which serve as a cloak for controlling businesses."

The US Ways and Means Committee reported: "Frequently families owning or controlling large businesses set up private trusts or foundations to keep control of the business in the family after death..."[3] The 1950 legislation left the term "foundation" undefined, but the subsequent 1969 definition of "private foundation" applied new restrictions to all charities.

A *Business Week* article published in 1960 captures the spirit of the times; it enthusiastically advocates the usefulness of a private foundation for tax avoidance and personal benefit. It recommends setting up a foundation if, "you have a sizable family business that you want to pass control of to your heirs, despite crippling Federal estate taxes". It goes on to report: "The real motive behind most private foundations is keeping control of wealth, even while the wealth itself is given away."[4]

Only expenditures that meet the definition of "qualifying distribution" count towards meeting the minimum payout rate of 5%.

---

[3] Thomas A. Troyer, *The 1969 Private Foundation Law: Historical Perspective on Its Origins and Underpinnings*, Council on Foundations, 2000, pp. 3–4.

[4] *Business Week*, 7 May 1960, p. 153. Quoted from Thomas A. Troyer, *The 1969 Private Foundation Law: Historical Perspective on Its Origins and Underpinnings*, Council on Foundations, 2000, p. 7.

The definition includes:

- Grants.
- Direct expenditures to accomplish charitable purposes (such as technical assistance to grantees).
- Charitable administrative expenses (such as for operating the foundation's grant programme).
- Amounts paid to acquire assets used directly to accomplish tax-exempt purposes (such as purchasing office furniture or computers).
- Programme-related investments.
- Certain amounts set aside for future charitable projects.

Taxes paid by a foundation do not count as qualifying distributions, but the foundations can claim such tax payments as a dollar-for-dollar credit towards meeting its 5% minimum distribution credit. Any expenses paid for managing investment assets do not count as qualifying distributions and do not provide any credit as in the case of taxes paid.

Author Carter Harrison describes the two critical financial issues affecting all foundations as deciding how to allocate assets and deciding how to spend assets: "For foundations wishing to adopt a spending policy that maximises current expenditures while preserving the purchasing power of their underlying assets, balancing these two issues efficiently and effectively can be daunting."[5]

The call for an increased payout rate

Equally daunting, if not more so, is the call for US foundations to increase their payout rate. In a highly controversial study, Perry Mehrling, under the auspices of the National Network of Grant-makers (NNG), makes a compelling case for an increase, despite the fact that several academics have subsequently dismissed his research

---

[5] Carter R. Harrison Jr, "It's how you slice it", *Foundation News & Commentary*, Council on Foundations, November/December 1999.

as flawed. He concluded: "A huge and mostly invisible element of the philanthropic field is more concerned with investment banking than grant-making."[6]

Mehrling maintains that the US Congress has achieved its goal in that the 1981 regulations that relaxed the minimum payout rate to 5% were intended to help private foundations rebuild their endowments. Rebuilding is complete. Total foundation assets have grown in real terms by almost three times since then. A typical foundation could have given away up to 8% of its assets during the past 20 years without significantly decreasing the value of its endowment.

In light of this, the sector is in danger of appearing to be exactly what the US Congress wanted to and probably still wants to prevent – that is, keeping tax-favoured foundations from becoming mere warehouses of wealth. Mehrling warns: "To the extent that individual foundations reduce payout to the legal minimum simply in order to increase their assets under management, they defeat the real social purpose of their privileged tax status and risk attracting renewed legislative attention."[7]

US debate signals trouble ahead

The debate in late autumn 2003 in the US House of Representatives over the Charitable Giving Act 2003 involved both Democrats and Republicans pushing for a measure that would prohibit foundations from counting administrative costs, such as rent or salaries, to meet

---

[6] Perry Mehrling, Barnard College, Columbia University, *Spending Policies for Foundations, The Case for Increased Grants Payout*, National Network of Grantmakers, 1999, p. 1.
[7] Ibid, p. 13.

the federal requirement of a 5% payout. In the end, the House did not change the payout rate, but, as William A. Schambra reports, the legislative skirmish over foundation policies could well be the harbinger of a new politics of philanthropy in which the right and left make more sustained and vigorous joint challenges to the orthodoxies of modern philanthropy as practised and preached by the nation's largest foundations:

> Most likely to come under attack: philanthropy's conviction that it brings to the table not just money to give away, but far more important, an objective, cumulative understanding of society's ills and the best ways to cure them. Challenges to the big foundations from left and right flanks are by no means new . . . but seldom, if ever, have they been mounted simultaneously.

The backdrop of the political attitudes over the years, whether left or right, has been coloured by a basic mistrust and suspicion, "that the large, modern foundations represent something anomalous in American democracy, namely the concentration of vast sums of wealth behind an aggressively pre-emptive claim to public policy expertise".

The debate over the payout rate goes much deeper than fiscal technicalities; it strikes at the very legitimacy of foundations. As Schambra explains, the dollars at stake hardly explain the reaction of foundations and politicians alike:

> By proposing to prohibit the counting of administrative costs in the payout calculation, lawmakers insultingly suggested that such expenses were merely non-charitable bureaucratic overheads, not the magnificent charitable offerings of wisdom that the large foundations insisted they were in their bid for democratic legitimacy.[8]

During the debates, Dorothy Ridings, President of the Council on Foundations, insisted, "foundations trade in two currencies: money and knowledge". This belief appears to be under attack, at least in the US. This is a sobering situation, as foundations strive to secure their position within increasingly complex societies in states where

---

[8] William A. Schambra, "The new politics of philanthropy", *The Chronicle of Philanthropy*, 13 November 2003, p. 37.

governments are under pressure to maintain their competitiveness on the global stage. Ralph R. Smith, Senior Vice-President of the Annie E. Casey Foundation, Baltimore, Washington, maintains that the work of foundations extends beyond simple grant-making as they use different methodologies to achieve their objectives, including advocacy, funding think tanks and convening stakeholders. Funds directed towards these methodologies are typically referred to as internal costs, which critics often point to as administrative expenses.

"Grants plus"

European foundations would do well to monitor the events unfolding across them. In an interview published in The McKinsey Quarterly,[9] Smith acknowledges that times are tough for foundations, and in the wake of media reports of mismanagement, excessive administrative costs, trustee fees and executive compensation, public concern is "understandable". However, he points out that big portfolio losses have reduced the grant-making of many foundations. At the same time, "in seeking to increase the payout rate indirectly by disallowing administrative and operating expenses, the legislation as originally drafted could negatively affect a number of important non-grant activities in which some foundations... are involved". He points to Casey's advocacy work on behalf of children as a case in point. (Casey has exceeded the 5% minimum payout rate in recent years.)

Smith maintains that Casey's work is "grants plus", which means much of the work is done behind the scenes, out of the public view. For this reason, foundations must do "a better job of explaining to everyone, including the media, the value of what they do". Because Casey's advocacy work is supported by good data, the foundation

---

[9] Les Silverman, "Building better foundations", The McKinsey Quarterly, 2004, Number 1, p. 95.

has invested $4.65 million a year in producing an annual report, *Kids Count Data*, which provides state-by-state data on key measures of children's well being. Its internal consulting group spends about $2 million a year advising state and local government agencies about welfare and juvenile-justice reforms. It also invests in technical assistance to support grantees and in peer assistance. In 2003, a considerable $16.5 million was invested in documentation and evaluation.

"Non-grant activities allow us to achieve results that otherwise would not be possible ... Part of the challenge now is trying to help the public and the policy-makers to understand that the contribution foundations ought not to be measured simply by how many grants are given in any year," he adds.

This is part of a wider debate as many – wrongly so – perceive the work of foundations to be limited to grant-making activities alone. This was discussed in Chapters 3 and 4.

The pros and cons

The issues spinning off the payout rate debate have long been the subject of controversy and the arguments for and against compelling on both sides. At the heart of the debate is the question: How much should be given away and how much should be saved for the future? How a foundation answers this question determines its strategy and supporting spending policies.

How much responsibility do we have for the next generation? In their interest, should money be spent today to alleviate what could become tomorrow's critical social challenges? Or not? The answers to these questions must be balanced with the issues of cost-effectiveness and efficiency. The answers are also critical to the political legitimacy of the foundation sector as it increasingly comes under scrutiny, particularly in view of corporate scandals and questions regarding charitable assets. These issues are coming to the forefront in the US, but they could just as easily surface in Europe.

The debate is coherently summarised by Akash Deep and Peter Frumkin. The authors set the stage by pointing out that America's 50 000 grant-making foundations control assets of $400 billion and disburse about $20 billion in grants each year to non-profit service providers. Foundation philanthropy continues to grow in size and is expected to explode as the baby-boom generation ages and declines. Some estimates have projected a $40 trillion transfer of wealth in the coming decades, with huge amounts flowing into foundations.

> Against this backdrop, two separate but narrow debates have raged in recent years about foundation grant-making and investment practices. The first debate has focused on finding ways to improve the way foundations make grants... The second debate has focused on locating the best financial strategy for the investment of endowment assets... There is, however, a more fundamental question that has largely been ignored, namely how much to give now and how much to save for future giving.[10]

The authors recommend revising the "old public policy" of the 5% minimum payout rate because its has "gone from being a floor when it was enacted... to a ceiling today". Frumkin also points out that the regulations drove up administrative costs and reduced the proportion of foundation assets going to charity. Administrative overhead in foundations rose from 6.4% in 1966 to 14.9% in 1972, where it has hovered ever since.[11]

Regulating foundation payouts involves tough trade-offs regarding current versus future charity. Michael Klausner writes in the *Stanford Social Innovation Review*:

> The lower the payout rate, the greater the amount saved and invested, and hence the greater the amount that can be distributed to future generations. Conversely, the higher the payout rate, the lower the amount available for future distribution. The arguments of those who advocate higher payout rates

---

[10] Akash Deep and Peter Frumkin, *The Foundation Payout Puzzle*, The Hauser Center for Nonprofit Organizations, The Kennedy School of Government, Harvard University, Working Paper No. 9, June 2001, p. 2.
[11] Peter Frumkin, "The ironies of foundation regulation", *The Chronicle of Philanthropy*, February 2004, p. 33.

amount to arguments that foundations should provide more money to current charity and less to future charity. Foundations that resist higher payout rates are in effect arguing for more future charity at the expense of current charity.[12]

Critical social problems should be addressed now

The concept of early intervention to address critical social problems now before they spiral out of control is popular with those advocating a higher payout rate for foundations. This strategy is preventative in that it allows foundations to actually address such problems at the root rather than treat the symptoms as they become increasingly acute.

Deep and Frumkin point to the obvious example of HIV/AIDS research in that funding work today has considerably more value than supporting research 20, 50 or 100 years from now. Klausner bluntly poses the question: "How much sacrifice should the current generation make so that future generations can have a cleaner environment, cheaper energy, better health and longer lives?"

He quotes Richard N. Goldman, co-founder of the Goldman Environmental Prize, when asked why the foundation pays out more than double the traditional 5%: "My 50 years in philanthropy have convinced me that, for the environment and other charitable causes, the 'rainy day' is upon us." Goldman maintains that the most urgent threat facing life in the twenty-first century is climate change. To this end, he believes:

> Now is the time to address the climate change issue head on, because the opportunity will never come again. If we do not act now, we will impose untold harm on future generations, and there will be nothing they can do to remedy the situation . . . People in the future will thank us if we act now.[13]

---

[12] Michael Klausner, "When time isn't money", *Stanford Social Innovation Review*, Spring 2003, p. 52.
[13] Ibid, pp. 56–57.

At the same time, there are funders and foundations that decide to spend their endowment over a longer period of time. For example, The Atlantic Philanthropies, founded by an Irish philanthropist, has several affiliate organisations in the US and Great Britain and is operating within a 20-year framework.

The intergenerational equity argument

The issue of society's responsibility to future generations has come to the fore in wide-ranging policy discussions world wide; it could be considered the backbone of the three-pillar concept of sustainable development. In the context of payout rates for foundations, it implies serious tax equity issues, particularly if Deep and Frumkin's prediction is correct concerning the exponential growth of foundation assets.

The favourable tax treatment of foundations results in the burden of lost tax revenue being borne by today's citizens. Yet the benefits of foundation-giving for the most part do not accrue to the taxpayers who make this expenditure. "By giving the wealthy the opportunity to create a foundation in perpetuity, taxpayers today are in essence being asked to subsidise the welfare of future generations, at a time when many current social needs continue to be unmet," the authors argue.

This "ever-evolving" intergenerational transfer of resources would be unproblematic if each generation made roughly equal tax expenditures, but this is clearly not the case. Deep and Frumkin point to the fact that as demographic waves of different sizes and different levels of resources age and transfer their wealth into foundations, the unequal intergenerational distribution of foundation assets will become pronounced.

At the same time, there is a case to be made for the fact that future generations are expected to contribute exponentially more to foundations (presuming the tax treatment does not change), in which case, why not insist upon a higher payout rate today to address urgent social and environmental problems that will only be exacerbated as time moves on and inequalities persist?

Maintain the status quo?

The authors cite equally persuasive arguments to maintain the current foundation payout rate, including:

- The realisation that social problems may get worse over time.
- The uncertainty posed by volatile financial markets.
- The weight of professional experience and tradition (pushing a foundation to adopt a higher payout requires overcoming the strong pull of the duty of care, which directs trustees to preserve assets for the future).
- The appearance of new problems that cannot at present be foreseen.
- The limitations of non-profit service organisations to effectively absorb sudden increases in funds.

Norman B. Ture, in a report prepared for the US Ad Hoc Committee examining the Internal Revenue Code, focuses on the impact of the (then) 6% payout rate with respect to the investment performance of foundations and their capacity to provide financial support for charities. The intent of the minimum distribution rule is to increase the amount of the foundations' distributions to charities. Yet in reality, he claims: "To the extent that public policy calls for a continuing and growing distribution capacity by foundations over the long term, a minimum distribution rule is counterproductive, irrespective of the total rate of return on foundation assets."

Ture asserts there is little factual justification for the notion that foundation payouts have been an inadequate return to society for the tax deductions society has given their donors: "Indeed, relatively few government spending programmes could meet the benefit–cost standards implied by foundation distributions in relation to tax savings to the donors of foundations' assets."[14]

---

[14] Norman B. Ture, *The Impact of the Minimum Distribution Rule on Foundations*, A report prepared for the Ad Hoc Committee on Section 4942, 5 April 1973, pp. 17 and 30.

Klausner notes that increasing the payout requirement to a level that would place foundations' perpetuity at risk could make the establishment of foundations less attractive to donors, which could result in less charity for both present and future generations.

Policy options

Deep and Frumkin outline two objectives when defining public policy. First, it should be demanding enough to ensure that foundations use their resources in ways that benefit the public, not just themselves. Second, public policy should be flexible enough to allow foundations to select a payout rate that is strategically aligned with their missions and the methodologies they use.

They suggest an inflation-adjusted variable payout rate keyed to foundation asset growth or a variable rate keyed to asset growth that is both adjusted for inflation and based on the average rate of return over several years. Public policy needs to be flexible enough to encourage foundations to "adopt a plurality of payout rates that are strategically aligned with the distinctive missions of individual foundations".

Deep and Frumkin finally conclude by conceding that regulating foundation payouts involves very tough trade-offs. However, they warn that in the search for a solution to the payout puzzle one thing should be clear: the long-standing 5% payout requirement has failed.

Smith advocates accountability. Casey holds itself accountable for three goals: impact, influence and leverage. What did an investment accomplish for the people whose lives they are hoping to affect? How are they better off? Who is behaving differently as a result of an investment? Are policy-makers, decision-makers, and opinion leaders saying different things, understanding different things and making different decisions? And finally, did the investment help to stimulate other investments? "Being focused on impact, influence and leverage forces us to establish milestones and benchmarks that allow us to track progress," he says.[15]

This conclusion holds an important lesson for European foundations. In light of trans-Atlantic developments, they should consider developing a self-regulating framework that would oblige them to pay out a fixed percentage annually. It is important for the sector to become proactive. In the European Commission's 1997 Communication concerning voluntary organisations and foundations in Europe, it emphasises the important role of civil society structures for future democratic development in Europe in reference to foundations and associations:

> Despite their increasing reliance on foundations and voluntary organisations to carry out a wide range of functions, public authorities have not on the whole acknowledged their responsibility to ensure that the sector is as well placed as possible to make its distinctive contribution to the public good.[16]

Why we need a payout rate in Europe

The events in the US, increasing public scrutiny and the inherent obligation that foundations have to create value for the societies in which they operate, are compelling reasons for the European foundation sector to initiate a proactive stance on the payout rate issue.

The European Commission called for a review of the sector by national authorities with a view to making proposals about what needs to be done to help the voluntary sector to increase its capacity. The existing policy vacuum may possibly be filled by well-intentioned public authorities, but this may not necessarily reflect what the foundation sector envisages for itself. A Europe-wide self-regulatory initiative setting standards for national preferential treatment and an average annual payout rate appears to be the best way forward in this situation.

---

[15] Ibid, p. 99.

[16] http://europa.eu.int/comm/enterprise/library/lib-social_economy/orgfd_en.pdf

The European Foundation Centre's legal and fiscal task forces have worked over the past years to build the information base and tools to help to enhance the operating frameworks of foundations and review legal and tax regimes governing foundations across the EU's 15 (now 25) member states. It has drafted a Model Law for Public Benefit Foundations in Europe, which serves as a template for law revisions at national level. It is also working on recommendations for an optional European statute to serve as a complementary legal form to national provisions for foundations.

Considering that foundations operate within a complex patchwork of national laws and regulations, it is natural to contemplate the development of a European framework, particularly as many work cross-border in partnership agreements (often partially funded by the European Commission) and as foundations extend their work into an enlarged European Union.

However, to date there has been little or no public debate on whether European foundations should be subject to a mandatory payout rate. The sector appears to be carefully sidestepping the issue.

The question the sector in Europe should be asking itself is whether this is enough to satisfy an increasingly engaged and critical public, and legislators seeking to fill an obvious policy vacuum. In particular, civil society organisations are becoming more involved in the charities and foundations that fund them. Politicians operating in environments characterised by different models of civil society will make different trade-offs, depending on the options available: should the initiative be publicly funded or should it be entrusted to a foundation exercising its tax preferential status?

Becoming more responsible

It is up to the sector to develop this efficiency, foster its diversity, and live up to its obligations as it redistributes societies' resources for the public good. For this reason, it is in the sector's interest to be more transparent, more accountable, and more effective; in other words, to become more responsible.

An important first step would be a self-imposed, 5%, inflation-averaged payout rate in the European foundation sector based on a fair definition of qualifying distribution and including non-grant-making activities.

This book makes an argument for an evolution of the ethics and professionalism of the philanthropic sector as a whole. This evolution into a new "ethic" should be founded on the values of transparency, accountability and responsibility. In Europe, this could be overseen by the European Foundation Centre. It can be argued that US foundations must do a much better job of explaining that they are not only about giving grants to the NGO sector and filling in the gaps left by a retreating state. They play very different, valuable roles in the societies in which they operate, for which they must deploy a broad spectrum of methodologies, as discussed in Chapters 3 and 4.

A higher payout rate stimulates economic development

Imposing some relatively high payout rate – or in the case of Europe, any rate at all – could effectively compel foundations to improve their investment performance by diversifying their portfolios and in this way contribute more to economic development.

Foundations with a low payout rate are usually more invested in bonds than in stocks because they require a lower return, which means that they can choose an asset portfolio with a lower risk and a consequent lower return objective (2.3%). As a result, they are investing more in government debt than contributing to the growth of the economies in which they operate. If a mandatory payout rate of about 5% were imposed, European foundations would be compelled to diversify.

A foundation's return objective determines its spending policy. For example, if the spending policy is 5%, the return objective is around 8%. This is primarily due to the investment management cost, but more importantly, to the expected rate of inflation (Table 5.1). If the rate of inflation were not taken into account, the endowment would lose value year after year.

The best way to achieve an average return of about 8% is through an asset allocation, a diversified portfolio which determines how much of the endowment is invested in which asset classes – stocks, bonds, foreign equities, real estate, and so on. Jeffrey R. Leighton, writing in *Foundation News & Commentary*, explains: "The goal of asset allocation is to identify efficient portfolios – combinations of investment assets that have the greatest probability of achieving the return objective with the least risk of any portfolio likely to achieve an equivalent return."[17]

Table 5.1   The point of low return

	Conservative Foundation	Aggressive Foundation
Spending policy as a percentage of assets	5.0%	5.5%
Endowment growth objective	0.0%	0.5%
Investment management costs	0.8%	1.0%
Pre-inflation return requirement	5.8%	7.0%
Expected rate of inflation	2.5%	3.0%
Return objective	8.3%	10.0%

From Jeffrey R. Leighton, *Foundation News & Commentary*, March/April 2003.

The above is accomplished through optimalisation models that rely heavily on historical data and relationships. For example, the asset allocation of the King Baudouin Foundation is shown in Table 5.2.

---

[17] Jeffrey R. Leighton, "Back to the basics", *Foundation News & Commentary*, March/April 2003, pp. 23–24.

Table 5.2 Portfolio Structure King Baudouin Foundation for an expected real return of 4.90% p.a.

Asset class	Index benchmark	Strategic weighting (%)	Target range (%)
European Equities	MSCI Europe	32	27–37
US Equities	Standard & Poor's 500	18	13–23
Far East Equities	80% Topix/20% FTSE AW Asia Pacific (ex India ex Japan ex Pakistan)	6	4–8
Emerging Equity Markets	MSCI Emerging Markets Free	4	2–6
>**Total Equities**	**Composite of the above Equity Benchmarks**	60	50–70
Global Corporate Bonds	1/3 Citigroup EuroBIG Corp Index/2/3 Citigroup WBIG USD Corp (Euro hedged)	15	12–18
European Government Bonds	Citigroup European GBI	25	20–30
Total Bonds	**Composite of the above Bond Benchmarks**	40	30–50
Property		0	—
Cash		0	—
TOTAL FUND	**Composite of all the above benchmarks**	100	—

Leighton points out that spending policy, the return objective and asset allocation are intrinsically linked. His "laws of linkage" merit consideration:

- Earning more means increasing the allocation to higher-return asset classes.
- Asset classes with higher expected returns are typically more volatile.
- Tolerance for volatility increases as the investment time horizon lengthens or if the foundation is able to adjust its spending policy.

It follows that the higher the payout rate, the more would foundations be forced to invest in equities, rather than government debt-related investments, further creating value by contributing to economic development.

Making a case for accountability

Amid all the furore raised by media revelations of foundation excesses – high trustee fees, self dealing, excessive compensation and other improprieties – the silence of the foundation community has been deafening. That is perhaps the greatest philanthropic scandal of all.

Boston Globe, 23 February 2004

This very strong opinion demonstrates that scrutiny, scepticism and hostility towards philanthropic institutions are on the rise in the US. Clearly, the issue of accountability (and hence legitimacy) cannot be resolved by a mandatory payout rate alone. The long-term health of the global foundation community will depend upon some drastic preventative medicine.

European foundations are not immune to such criticism. Articles published in France and the Netherlands, for example, signal serious rumblings about exercising more control over the sector. Such reactions are related to the US scandals, but also to the revelation in the wake of 11 September that "cover up" the suggestion that foundations could be funding terrorist activities. This erupted against the backdrop of the massive growth of the sector throughout the 1990s and the lack of government control and enforcement capacity. They have focused public attention on the sector, which is now coming under heavy fire by the public, policy-makers and opinion leaders.

The only way to address these critical issues is for the sector to be proactive and develop codes of practice and governance standards. As important would be the agreement upon a mechanism whereby such principles could be imposed and enforced. In Europe, this could be the European Foundation Centre (EFC) and in the US, the Council on Foundations.

In the US, the Council on Foundations is calling for grants from its members to fund a two-year programme 2004–2005, Building Strong and Ethical Foundations: Doing it Right, whereby it intends to develop new guiding principles and governance standards that reflect in more specificity the existing principles for effective grant-making to which all members subscribe. In addition, it will step up professional development, materials and outreach about legal and ethical governance practices to foundation professionals as well as state and federal charity officials.

This self-regulation and self-governance is necessary to the sector in Europe, but perhaps not sufficient. The European Union and its various member states should be more attentive and, in cooperation with organisations such as the EFC, develop an enabling regulatory framework to better address the governance of foundations.

6

From strategy to implementation

The goal of the impact-driven foundation – to effect meaningful change or to act as an effective convenor – can be achieved by deploying the full range of methodologies available. However, foundations must work within a strategic implementation framework that does not stifle innovation. Consultants specialising in organisational change and development apply various formulas designed to initiate, navigate and manage change. In practice, however, the challenge for a foundation is to push beyond such theoretical frameworks to find the right mix of methodologies to achieve its goals – both within the long-term strategic framework and in day-to-day project implementation.

The paradox of change lies in its very nature: an organisation must change to change. To best illustrate this more technical aspect of the strategy and implementation of foundation work, this chapter and the next focus on the work of the King Baudouin Foundation (KBF). Many other foundations have undergone or are going through a similar process in their quest to create value.

The KBF needed a new internal structure, adapted financial resources, a clear set of operational management tools and a process of continuous evaluation, control and feedback. The challenges inherent in successfully managing organisational change are much greater than the practicalities involved in making it happen. It involves a profound cultural shift within the organisation and a commitment to ongoing reflection, learning and risk-taking. (The latter being somewhat of an anathema to most foundations.) It also requires the courage to abandon projects and programmes that do not work, regardless of external pressures.

Another paradox lies in the concept of "managing change". Continuous innovation and "change management" are fundamental to the success of the impact-driven foundation. However, to avoid the dangers implicit in strategic planning – which is often rigid, defined by deliverables, and constrained by milestones carved in stone – a careful balance must be struck between discipline and systematisation, innovation and creativity, intuition and entrepreneurship, change and continuity.

In 2001–2002, KBF developed a strategic management model with a view to optimising its performance by being more effective and flexible – thus creative and innovative – within a new framework that better reflects its mission, vision and values. The framework reflects its decentralised "matrix" model, whereby it strives to make all significant organisational information transparent and available, raising levels of involvement, thus improving decision-making across the organisation.

During the process, which closely involved consultation with employees and stakeholders, KBF:

- Developed strategic policy options.
- Defined its mission, vision and values.
- Examined its activities and clustered them into four programme areas.
- Clearly outlined its objectives, policies and programmes.
- Restructured responsibility across the organisation.
- Redesigned its project management cycle.

Determining the strategy

The development of a strategic management process meant analysing how to optimise performance through achieving impact in an effective and efficient way. To KBF, this involves producing change and being recognised for it. It also means achieving goals and targets through a specific approach that uses as few human and financial resources as possible.

To determine its role, KBF relies on society as a whole, the general public, decision-makers and those who receive support (partners and grantees). The Board of Governors makes the final decision on the strategy. KBF is accountable to the general public as it operates in an advantageous tax environment and receives considerable funding from the National Lottery.

A representative survey of the Belgian population, which included 100 decision-makers, was the starting point for formulating the strategy. Through an interactive, participatory process involving internal staff and external consultants, the mission, vision and values were developed as well as objectives, policies and programmes. In the approach, certain principles were defined as the backbone of developing the proposed strategic management model:

- External stakeholder involvement.
- Strong participation of employees.
- Limited and focused external consultancy.
- Fixed timeframes.
- Well-defined deliverables.
- Clear decision procedures.
- Continuous feedback.

A SWOT (strengths, weaknesses, opportunities and threats) analysis took into consideration societal evolutions in the environment within which KBF works, its positioning and stakeholders' expectations, including partners and beneficiaries. The strengths and weaknesses of activities at the time – as well as the foundation's vision, objectives and strategies – were also analysed. The analysis included an employee survey, external stakeholder in-person interviews and a desk analysis by external international consultants.

A management dilemma

"The impact-driven foundation" chapter makes an argument for using the different methodologies a foundation has at its disposal to make an optimal impact. Not every societal problem or issue requires the complete toolbox. Which tools or methods are deployed depends on several factors, such as the level of control the foundation has over an issue and the diversity of partners engaged in solving the particular problem.

Therein lies a management dilemma: striking the right balance between methodologies. When determining which methodologies are the most relevant, management must consider both efficacy and efficiency. The latter consideration will help to answer questions about whether the foundation is giving grants for advocacy purposes or to engage in advocacy itself.

These considerations involve trade-offs between the number of staff a foundation is ready to support in relationship to its budget, taking into account growing salary costs and other overhead costs. Also important is the loss of flexibility incurred when the organisation decides to become completely operational.

No guidelines or benchmarks exist for determining the right balance between grant-giving and other methodologies. In finding a good balance between labour- and capital-intensive methodologies, KBF tries to maintain a mix of 60% grant-giving (excluding personnel costs) and 40% on the other methodologies as described in Chapters 3 and 4.

In addition, there are considerations more linked to a foundation's theory of change and which role is envisioned for civil society organisations it engages with. Some foundations view NGOs both as the real actors at grassroots level and as pressure groups at a higher level. For this reason, they believe that funding civil society organisations is the way forward. Others believe that this sector is not always a credible actor and does not have the capacity to achieve the desired impact. As a result, they prefer to do the work themselves.

The jury is still out...

Developing strategic policy options

In defining KBF's mission, vision and values, strategic policy options were outlined, with a view towards narrowing the foundation's work down to four strategic areas: social justice, civil society, governance and promoting contemporary philanthropy. As a result, KBF was positioned as a foundation that:

- Concentrates on a limited number of action fields.
- Wants to increase its European dimension.
- Intends to think more strategically in terms of methods and to become a learning organisation, involving impact evaluation and knowledge sharing inside and outside the foundation.
- Pays particular attention to cultural diversity and the gender dimension.
- Keeps 15% of the budget free on an annual basis, allowing the foundation to be flexible enough to react quickly to new societal challenges and opportunities.

Defining mission, vision and values

Reviewing and discussing the strategic policy options enabled the foundation to come to a clearer definition of its mission, vision and values.

- *Mission*: To help to improve the living conditions of the population.
- *Vision*: The foundation wants to encourage all the different players in society to be committed to working together to bring about lasting changes that will promote justice, democracy and development.
- *Values*: The King Baudouin Foundation is a public benefit foundation seeking to serve society and promote solidarity. It is an independent, pluralistic institution that respects diversity. It is concerned about quality, and strives to carry out its activities in a spirit of transparency and integrity.

One mission: four programmes

Social justice   This programme identifies new forms of social injustice and supports initiatives to give more autonomy to vulnerable people. The programme covers three areas of activity:

- New forms of social injustice – through the Listening Network.
- Migration.
- Safety and insecurity.

Civil society   This programme encourages citizens to become involved and helps to strengthen associations. The programme is designed to encourage citizens to become involved in society and to increase the impact of their initiatives. It includes four areas of action:

- Improving the impact and quality of associations.
- Increasing individuals' social involvement.
- Promoting citizen participation at local level.
- Encouraging cultural pluralism.

Governance   In this area, initiatives are aimed at involving citizens more closely in decisions regarding developments in science and the way in which goods and services are produced and consumed. The programme is designed to increase the impact that citizens can have on the debate and decision-making process. Citizens' concerns and the questions they raise in this regard deserve particular attention. The programme involves three areas of activity:

- Science and technology.
- Production, consumption and trade.
- Acquisition of experience with participatory debating methods and decision-making processes.

Funds and contemporary philanthropy   This programme encourages modern forms of generosity, provides information to donors and offers them a range of tools to engage in philanthropy. The programme is designed to encourage generosity in society and covers three areas of activity:

- Developing research on philanthropy.
- Raising donors' awareness and providing information.
- Promoting and managing tools to support philanthropy.

The strategic management model

This strategic management model (Figure 6.1) is implemented across the organisation. It defines KBF's overarching approach and provides a flexible framework within which to achieve the projects within the four programmes.

Managing the change – making it work

KBF's management model depends on a workable strategic plan, together with an adapted structure. It also involves adapted financial resources, operational management tools and a system for evaluation, control and feedback. Operational management tools must be honed if change is to be effected efficiently and effectively. KBF's toolkit includes knowledge management, competence management, project management and communication.

It was clear from the beginning that it would be a mistake to structure everything around financial transactions; there was also a need to think about the foundation's broader role when implementing the plan.

Towards becoming a "knowledge foundation"

Knowledge is an invaluable asset in the process of bringing about societal change. Nevertheless, foundations traditionally think in terms of how their funding can bring about change. Lucy Bernholz and Kendall Guthrie write that most foundations have barely begun to tap their information assets:

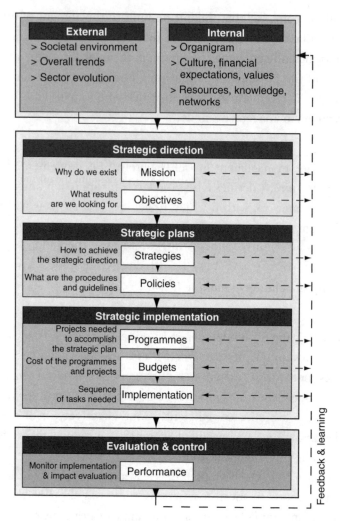

Figure 6.1 Strategic management model

Those funders that can transform the information flowing through their doors into knowledge – and then get it out to the people and organizations in the field who can apply it – can significantly expand their influence. We call funders that do this well "knowledge foundations".[1]

---

[1] Lucy Bernholz and Kendall Guthrie, "Knowledge is an asset, too", *Foundation News & Commentary*, May/June 2000, p. 28.

The authors point out that there is no limit to the amount of information a foundation can distribute and that the more times a knowledge asset is applied, the greater is the return on the initial investment.

KBF and the European Foundation Centre initiated a survey[2] on knowledge management in 2003, in which one formal definition was identified:

> Knowledge management comprises the activities focused on the organisation of gaining knowledge from its own experience and from the experience of others, and on the judicious application of that knowledge to fulfil the mission of the organisation.

These activities are executed by marrying technology, organisational structures and cognitive based strategies to raise the yield of existing knowledge and produce new knowledge. Concretely, knowledge management is about:

- Knowing what interesting projects there are in the foundation's domain.
- Creating networks to learn from each other.
- Sharing useful information with others.
- Bringing grantees together to enable them to learn from each other.

The challenge lies in managing and sharing knowledge and learning, which requires follow-up and evaluation, as well as application. This is an iterative process that demands not only a supportive IT structure but also clearly defined internal procedures that enable the acquisition and filtering of content.

At KBF, projects and initiatives are evaluated upon their effectiveness – what worked and what did not – as well as upon whether they contributed to the organisation's overall strategic objectives as defined within the foundation's four programme areas. (This is explained in detail in Chapter 7.)

---

[2] KBF and the European Foundation Centre, *Knowledge Management: Where Foundations in Europe Stand and Wish to Go For*, April 2004.

Essential to success in this area is fostering a collaborative and learning culture within the organisation. KBF's knowledge management originates from project templates that include an evaluation component. This information is disseminated across the organisation and complemented by a daily exchange of information through the sharing of news, external reports and conference outcomes. The Internet is an invaluable tool that presents new opportunities for organisations to share information and knowledge both internally and externally.

This explicit knowledge is complemented by tacit knowledge, which is more difficult to share among colleagues. Innovative ideas are fostered through developing "coins" (a community of interest around issues), which subsequently leads to new projects and new contacts.

It is also essential to recognise, admit and learn from mistakes. This requires a foundation to take risks and be courageous in the face of often-critical stakeholders looking for immediate impact and measurable results. Efficient information management is thus an asset that creates change through knowledge, which then becomes another leverage point for such change.

The joint KBF and European Foundation Centre survey on knowledge management[3] reported that, among other things, all respondents wish to improve on their toolkit (Figure 6.2). An important recommendation of the survey is that foundations should consider creating a "who knows what" structure of exchange of knowledge on a European level.

Competence management

As Nadya K. Shmavonian writes in a paper for the International Network on Strategic Philanthropy,[4] programme professionals are the

---

[3] Ibid.

[4] Nadya K. Shmavonian, *Management Practices surrounding Program Professionals in US and European Foundations*, International Network on Strategic Philanthropy, http:// www.insp.efc.be.

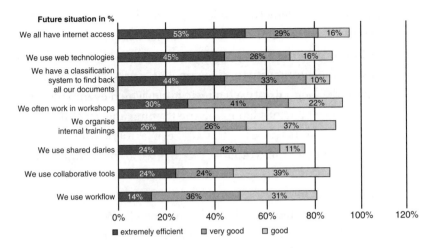

Figure 6.2   Foundations' strategy on knowledge management

"engines of implementation" in staffed foundations. Together with money and knowledge, human resources is a critical resource. As a result, an effective human resources strategy is a key to their success.

Many challenges confront the foundation world in this area. The remuneration policy is important, but so are working conditions, such as flexible work hours (part-time, working from home, sabbatical leaves) and personal development and training opportunities. A major challenge is attracting competent people in the face of competition from better-paid positions in the private sector. At KBF, a private firm conducts the staff benchmarking: employees are paid 5% less than that paid to professionals in general.

People who work for foundations are not motivated solely by remuneration, but also by their engagement in work that helps to resolve societal problems. The tension in this area, however, cannot become too strong, especially if one wants to engage staff with financial and management skills, as their skills are highly portable. Creating an attractive work environment while maintaining staff motivation and productivity is another challenge. There is a tendency in the foundation sector, particularly in Europe, that once staff is hired, they do not move out of their jobs quickly. As a result, lack of turnover is an issue.

There is a risk of people becoming less open to change and a deficit of fresh ideas and creative approaches to new challenges.

At KBF, the remuneration policy is also tied to an appraisal that includes a 360-degree evaluation every four years and a personal assessment at the beginning of a strategic cycle, which eventually leads to a personal development plan involving training and coaching.

All these elements are essential to keep a foundation vibrant, animated and what Shmavonian describes as a "breathing organisation".

Two other difficult tensions exist within foundations. The first is the tension of being an engaged, passionate and effective advocate for the projects being run, but at the same time crossing the line to become an activist. The latter can jeopardise a foundation's role as a catalyst of change and convenor.

Second, there are different schools of thought on what a foundation needs most: specialists or generalists. What impact-driven foundations primarily need is staff with good project management and team skills, an insight into different theories of social and political change, and good interpersonal and diplomatic skills to play the convenor and facilitator roles. Specialists can be brought in more on a case-by-case basis and can be part of the external team linked to a project.

Project management

Projects within the four programme areas go through a rigorous process, from their inception through to the evaluation and "lessons learned" stage. Project templates include background, description, target groups, deliverables, impact, critical success factors, evaluation, communication, management, budget, planning and phases (Figure 6.3).

The management team submits the project to the Board of Governors. Once approved the management team's "go–no go" system analyses whether or not it meets specific criteria. Evaluation is a critical component of this process. Evaluation at the "go–no go" stage examines

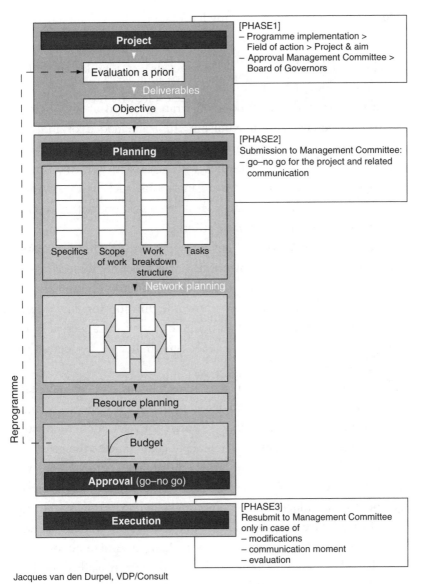

Jacques van den Durpel, VDP/Consult

Figure 6.3 The project cycle

specific goals and desired effects. It is very important to describe the desired output (deliverables) and outcome (impact) as specifically as possible. By engaging in an evaluation of the project, the programme and the foundation itself demonstrates its relevance and value to society – as well as its vulnerability and failings.

Communication

As discussed in Chapter 4, the impact-driven foundation will not succeed if it doesn't communicate what it is trying to accomplish. KBF uses a two-pronged communication strategy aimed at enhancing its institutional image and maximising the value-added of individual projects. It deploys the conventional tools – newsletters, agendas, annual reports and a website – together with a proactive media strategy, developed with various partner organisations, such as the European Policy Centre. The institutional image communication strategy is pinned to both linguistic and geographic criteria.

Much has been written about why it is critical that foundations engage in strategic communication that is precisely targeted as well as sensitive and appropriate to cultural contexts. Making the case for strategic communications as an underpinning for effective and efficient philanthropy is not difficult. In many instances, it is critical, particularly as they try to meet the challenges associated with value creation.

The difficult issue, however, is deciding when not to communicate – an equally strategic and critical decision. In some instances, communication could impede a foundation's convenor role. Some foundations have been accused of being too humble to communicate their successes. But in some instances, this humility is invaluable. For example, while tuning into social justice issues, the KBF's Listening Network identified specific problems faced by migrants in Belgium's prison system. Not only do they face language issues, but it was discovered that while incarcerated, their legal status remains unchanged. As a result, once they are released, they are "warehoused" in a detention facility until residency issues are resolved. Why not resolve this legal question while they are incarcerated? A decision was made not to widely publicise these findings as it could have worked against KBF's overarching goal of the Migrations and New Hospitalities initiative to create a more positive public attitude towards migrants.

Working towards continuous innovation

How does a leader distinguish between "need" (which never ends) and "opportunity" (where lasting change might result)? How does a leader hang on to qualitative contributions and not sacrifice those to quantitative measurement?[5]

KBF's practice of being flexible within its strategic management model intends to provide for continuous innovation. By the focused restructuring of its operations, the foundation has embraced its philosophy of "change to change". This is a learning process, but the seeds of change are starting to bear fruit. The actual strategic framework has been implemented and it appears that its impact and added value is repositioning the foundation into its true "hybrid" role. This better enables it to tackle some of the challenges ahead.

To move forward in programming, it is essential to have an exit plan at the appropriate time – such as KBF did with the Architectural Heritage Programme by handing it over to the NGOs that the foundation helped to create. In this regard, it is important to understand at which point involvement can smother and stifle the creativity of the very organisation(s) the foundation is seeking to empower. Co-dependency is a negative dynamic that in the end damages both parties. In entering new programme areas, it is important to bring in new expertise to give a fresh perspective to the organisation's long-term and short-term goals.

When piloting an organisation through change, a leader must continuously seek answers to these questions. It takes both time and courage to overcome resistance to change by those within the organisation, its stakeholders and shareholders. It takes strong – and often lonely leadership – to navigate the uncharted waters of organisational insecurity. Communication is essential during this process, as is fostering a culture that at once respects and stimulates a participatory process.

---

[5] Excerpted from *Leadership in Challenging Times*, a discussion paper prepared for participants at the 2004 Council on Foundations Annual Conference.

7

Evaluation: The bedrock of accountability

Almost everyone would agree that NGOs and other actors in the non-profit sector should be accountable and transparent. This holds particularly true for foundations, endowed with a special, privileged place in society because of their tax favoured status. This "accountability squeeze" (so-named by mainstream media over the past few years) is one of the major challenges facing foundations today.

In the face of charges of "cheating foundations" (another media label in the reporting of several unsavoury incidents of malfeasance in the sector), Dorothy Ridings, President and CEO of the Council on Foundations (USA), launched a major initiative in 2004 aimed at governance and stewardship, calling for intensified professional development and outreach about strong legal and ethical govern-ance practices to foundation professionals, advisers and government officials.

That the sector is officially responding more pragmatically to the call for accountability and transparency is an extremely positive step. But the question remains: How to do it? Accountability to donors, stakeholders, grantees, board members and the general public as to how funds are spent is a part of everyday business, as is compiling informa-tion about individual projects or programmes. Today's challenge goes beyond standardised reporting forms and the collection of reams of data – adding up grant totals does not result in a sum that evaluates a foundation's impact.

Proving that foundations "do good" is a formidable task, for how can societal impact be measured? How can foundations ensure that their work is making a difference? Some have rejected performance measurements, standardised forms and practices, relying instead on narratives and personal accounts from beneficiaries. Others are engaging in a form of benchmarking.

Foundations are being called upon to demonstrate their performance, but this can only be accomplished by compiling solid evidence provided by careful evaluation. This process in itself raises a myriad of questions, but the main ones are:

- Who should do the evaluation? Those within the organisation, some type of watchdog organisation, an independent institution such as a university, or another actor from the burgeoning evaluation industry?
- What should be evaluated? Project or programme accomplishments, the effect on beneficiaries, or numbers/statistics?
- How should it be evaluated?
- How should the results be reported?
- How can the impact be best evaluated?

The last question is the most difficult to answer, but it is also the most critical if foundations are to fulfil their purpose of value creation. The King Baudouin Foundation (KBF) has developed what we believe is an understandable and usable conceptual framework for evaluation to assist it in concretely implementing the evaluative components of its projects and programmes.

The following is a synthesis of this methodology, as presented in *Evaluation: A Means to Better Actions and a Greater Level of Societal Accountability*, a working paper prepared in May 2004.[1]

---

[1] Tinne Vandensande, Patricia Van Houtte, Jean-Pierre Goor, Frieda Lampaert and Guy Redig, *Evaluation: A Means to Better Actions and a Greater Level of Societal Accountability*, King Baudouin Foundation, May 2004.

Evaluation: exploring a concept

Evaluation is a process of learning on the way to better action and provides basic information for the societal justification of and responsibility for a foundation's actions. The process of learning in this context means the systematic analysis of, and reflection upon, actions and activities (such as a project or a programme) to test their value and improve them.

Evaluation is a central aspect of project management, which requires an attitude of learning and checking. This attitude is and should be continuously present. Evaluation is also a specific component or phase, which must be allocated a distinct place; it must be concrete, tangible and visible. In addition, the evaluation must also be able to be evaluated. At KBF, evaluation is primarily a component of project management, but is also designed to stimulate an evaluative attitude.

What or whom can be evaluated?

An evaluation can focus on almost all aspects of the foundation:

- The evaluation of a part of a project – for example, the communication, the functioning of the jury, the quality of the supporting associations.
- The evaluation of the project as a whole, with emphasis on the results of the project, such as deliverables and impact.
- The evaluation at the level of the domain of action or a cluster of projects from different programmes that are collected around a common subject.
- The evaluation of a programme.
- The evaluation of the foundation as a whole.

As the evaluation departs from the project level and moves via the domain of action and programme to the foundation as a whole, the accent also shifts from the earlier concern for deliverables to impact assessment (Figure 7.1).

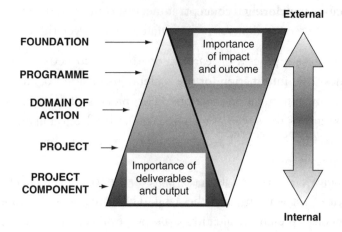

Figure 7.1   What the different interests evaluate

It is important that project managers pay explicit attention to the levels of domain of action and programme in their evaluations (Figure 7.2). Project evaluation is a basis for the evaluation of the initiative, programme and foundation; however, the whole is always more than the sum of its parts.

As described in Chapter 6 ("From strategy to implementation") the management team submits a project to the Board of Governors. If it is given a green light, the management team has a "go–no go" system

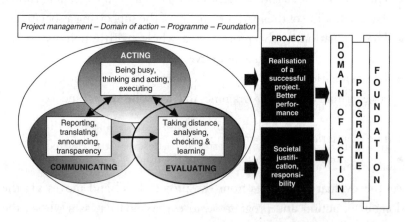

Figure 7.2   Evaluation's place within the project system and the foundation

in place to analyse whether or not it meets specific criteria. Evaluation is a specific component of project management, yet there are clear linkages to the level of domain of action and programme, and to the foundation as a whole.

Always and everywhere?

It appears that internal evaluation must occur always and everywhere; with each project/programme, a deliberate dwelling on both monitoring and evaluation must occur. This is not true for explicit, rather compli-cated, external evaluations. Here the question must be asked: Is this worth the effort? It is important to pay attention, among other things, to the following elements:

- A new or innovative approach.
- The threat of routine and predictability.
- Major societal turbulence.
- The intuitive sense that something is missing.
- A specific moment in the policy cycle of the foundation, for example when creating a new strategic plan.

Critical success factors

The success of an evaluation is largely dependent upon the clarity and focus with which the project was developed. If no specific goals or desired effects were established, it is almost impossible to estimate the value of such. Therefore, it is critical to describe the desired output (deliverables) and outcome (impact) in the project file ("go–no go") as intelligently as possible.

At the same time, it is important to state that a project or programme may also have unexpected side-effects. These can be positive, neutral or negative and could result in unexpected spin-offs.

During the evaluation process, it is also necessary to look for these effects.

The tension between vulnerability and responsibility

Evaluation is about calling oneself and one's own actions into question. This requires an attitude of vulnerability. Vulnerability can be dangerous and can undermine the strength of the project, the programme or the foundation. Evaluation occupies a space between power and weakness and/or between vulnerability and responsibility.

By engaging in evaluation, the project/programme/foundation hopes to demonstrate its relevance and value to society, but at the same time reveals its vulnerability and failings. Because this equilibrium is so difficult to obtain, external communication of the results of the evaluation requires particular attention. There is a risk that, out of the tension between vulnerability and responsibility, a fear of failure becomes so prominent that entrepreneurial approaches and intuitive actions are buried and cannot be expressed.

Common sense and intuition

Evaluation in the KBF context is not a scientific exercise. Inspired by scientific qualities, evaluation is primarily an exercise with a pragmatic rather than a theoretical aim. The goal is and remains "improvement and legitimatisation" of concrete action. Despite the existence of many, sometimes complex, instruments, it is primarily common sense and intuition that counts, namely, the results must be worth the effort invested. The professionalism of the project worker plays an important role in almost every choice made during the project cycle.

Evaluating cost

An evaluation always requires energy and, as a result, money. The scale of these costs depends, among other things, on the following:

- The importance attached to the evaluation. New, experimental or risky projects can justify a higher cost.
- The cost must always be seen in relation to the total cost of the project. There are no fixed percentages that can be applied.
- The most important guiding principle is common sense.

The introduction of external evaluators and the use of complex methods of evaluation are very expensive, and this method can only be defended when there is a great possibility of value being added.

An evaluation cycle

To evaluate, choices must be made, and there are several dimensions to the decision-making process:

- *First phase*: Is this project (component) or programme worth the effort of evaluation? A "no" to this question excludes additional evaluative action; a "yes" signals the beginning of an evaluation cycle.
- *Second phase*: Fundamental choices are faced regarding performing the evaluation. What are we going to evaluate (and why), when, for whom and the choice of an evaluation method. In making these choices, KBF uses an evaluation matrix to obtain as concrete results as possible to answer: What do we want to know and why?
- *Third phase*: The results of the evaluation must be understandable and be formulated and presented in a manageable way. There are always two types of results: How can we perform better in the future? How responsible was our action, and can we justify it? That is, lessons learned.

- *Fourth phase*: The results of the communication element of the evaluation is a strategic issue to be dealt with in consultation with colleagues on the project team, communications and management.
- *Fifth phase*: How could things have been done differently? Was the evaluation carried out satisfactorily?

Many concepts, many dimensions

Evaluation can be discussed using many concepts and in many dimensions.

- *Monitoring*: a continuous and systematic follow-up of the process in progress. In effect, continuous data collection.
- *Evaluation*: interpreting the data, making value judgements, expressing appreciation.

A distinction should also be made among the different types of "facts":

- *Objective facts*: a collection of numbers, percentages, counting and measuring.
- *Subjective facts*: looking for and articulating opinions, convictions, and views.

The differences between:

- *The process*: the method of production.
- *The product*: that which is concretely produced at the end of a process.

The different kinds of "results":

- *Output*: concrete products, deliverables.
- *Outcome*: the influence on social reality, on society.

Evaluations can be conducted in different "directions", including:

- Directed inside – towards oneself: to one's own, internal and closed system (inner-directed or directed inside).

- Directed outside – towards others: for the outside world, those external to the foundation.
- Differences in the type of involvement of the target group being evaluated need to be considered. Two major distinctions can be made:
  - (a) The "below the line target group" – those people and/or groups already active or involved in the project, for example, those who submit files, all those selected, members of the jury, and supervisors or external experts. Members of this group are close to the subject being evaluated and, as a result, require a specific evaluation instrument.
  - (b) The "above the line target group" – those people and/or groups who were not actively involved with the subject being evaluated but were nevertheless involved in some way, for example, people/groups who submitted no file, experts or specialised institutions not actively involved. Their distance from the subject being evaluated is greater but their knowledge of the subject is nevertheless important. The members of this group are very important to an evaluation, with respect to questions regarding why they did not participate, how they perceived the project, and so on. The "above the line" group can be very extensive. A specific evaluation instrument is also appropriate in this instance.
- The different proximities of the evaluator is also an important consideration. The choice lies between doing it oneself and having it done externally. In the latter instance, the ownership issue is critical.

Defining impact

The essential, overarching goal of projects, programmes and KBF as a whole is having an impact by effecting societal change. Evaluating impact is not a simple exercise. When defining impact for KBF's evaluation methodology working paper, the authors drew upon work done under the TAMI project.[2] Put simply, if one actor (the foundation) does something, it is undertaken with the intention of changing something, preferably to improve it. The activity must therefore make a difference, preferably a positive one and in the desired direction. The activity leads to change. If this change is the result of the activity, then there has been an impact.

A definition: *Impact is every change in the area of knowledge, policy, opinions or actions by relevant actors in the societal debate on* (fill as appropriate).

In an evaluation, KBF asks the following questions:

- Was there an impact?
- What has changed and in what direction?
- Was the change in direction the desired one, did we achieve what we intended with respect to change?
- Was the impact clearly the result of foundation's activity?
- Was the change brought about by the foundation, or were there other causes (causality)?

The three types of impact shown in Figure 7.3 and Table 7.1 are very different and may be carefully expressed as a hierarchy in which, for example, a change in attitude indicates a stronger impact than an increase in knowledge. In some cases, a measure taken can result in serious structural change and thus perhaps create sustainable impact.

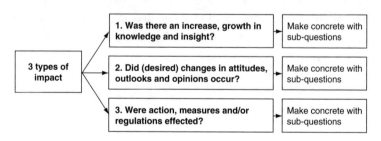

Figure 7.3   Three types of impact

---

[2] Leonhard Hennen, Sergio Bellucci, Robby Berloznik, David Cope, Laura Cruz Castro, Theo Karapiperis, Lars Klüver, Miltos Liakopoulos, Luis Sanz Mendez, Jan Staman, Susanne Stephan and Tomasz Szapiro, *Towards a Framework for Assessing the Impact of Technology Assessment*, TAMI, Technology Assessment in Europe: Between Method and Impact.

Table 7.1 Three basic questions and sub-questions about impact

Impact 1	Impact 2	Impact 3
Does our action/intervention result in more knowledge and insight on . . .	*Does our action/intervention result in a change in opinions, outlooks and attitudes among the target groups?*	*Does our activity/intervention result in action and measures being taken?*
• Were technical and other aspects made more clear and understandable?	• Was an influence realised on the political agendas?	• Did new forms of interactive policy arise?
• Did a more cohesive image of the topic emerge?	• Did the level of public debate increase?	• Did the level of public involvement increase?
• Did the consequences and results of a number of interventions become clearer?	• Did the level of self-reflection on the part of the actors involved increase?	• Did reactions occur that led to change, and if so, which changes, by/for whom, how?
• Did a more clear policy analysis emerge?	• Were the bottlenecks handled better and possibly eliminated?	• Was the change translated into sustainable structures, regulations, laws, etc.?
• Did more of those involved become a part of the picture? Did the network around the topic become clear?	• Was the policy network expanded and strengthened?	
• Were new visions and scenarios developed and made useable?	• Is there more cohesiveness present in the policy?	
	• Did the public evaluate the policy, bringing about a greater level of democratic legitimisation for this policy?	

(TAMI)

A holistic approach

KBF gives grants to various neighbourhood projects with the aim of being a catalyst to create partnerships among citizen initiatives, local authorities and local businesses. These projects, funded from the foundation's programmes (social justice, civil society, governance and promoting philanthropy) range from integrating migrant communities, creating safer neighbourhoods and restoring historical buildings, to poverty alleviation.

Each project could be evaluated separately, but in this case, the foundation decided upon a cluster evaluation to gauge the overall impact of projects on each neighbourhood. A survey was done at grantee level that also included local initiatives not selected for funding by KBF. This also resulted in a cartographic picture of supported projects at country level.

The result of this approach is a valuable insight into where and in which neighbourhoods the foundation is present. When this information is combined with socioeconomic and demographic data of the neighbourhoods, it reveals whether the foundation is funding those with the most needs and demonstrates impact. In addition, clustering the evaluation gives KBF insight into whether it is better to give overall strategic grants or to continue with the traditional scattered approach – a clear value-added to future planning.

Methods of evaluation

The ambitions of KBF's approach to evaluation are not distinctly scientific; however, the methods chosen are practical and easy to understand, using a mix of quantitative and qualitative methodologies. The two are not incompatible, but complementary. It is not always necessary to use them together, as one sometimes works better than the other; however, in KBF's experience, they usually work well in tandem.

The quantitative approach, dealing with figures, has advantages and disadvantages, as experience in the foundation world has shown.

Generally there are a number of basic figures that provide a very rudimentary view of what has occurred. If possible it is important from the start of the project – with the deliverables – to specify figures (for example, number of intended support interventions, number of intended participants, number of intended activities, scope of the intended support, intended print run for folders, publication, etc.).

A quantitative approach lends itself more to evaluating the output, but it can also be filled in with qualitative elements.

A qualitative approach, being abstract, is more difficult. How can we best capture quality? Assessing quality involves several approaches, each with advantages and disadvantages. These are well documented in existing research and background materials and include seeking opinions and views through questionnaires, working with preferred witnesses, and structured dialogues.

Whichever methodology or combination of methodologies is used, the material brought together must ultimately be translated into concrete, clear and usable conclusions designed to improve performance (Figure 7.4). The result of the evaluation lies in new learnings, allowing the foundation to function more effectively and efficiently and to better argue its societal responsibility more clearly, using supporting evidence.

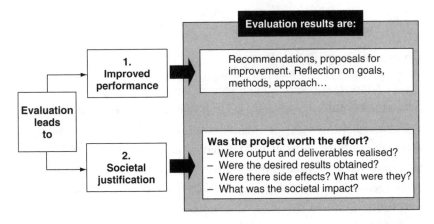

Figure 7.4   Process and results of evaluation

Driven by the numbers: a risky business

The sector tends to gravitate towards the easy solution – that is, to base too many evaluations on strong, black-and-white quantitative factors. This number-driven approach is surely an invaluable starting point in many instances, but there lies an inherent danger in over-emphasising the importance of, or relying on, numbers.

First, it could push foundations into launching only those initiatives that promise measurable results. This poses the risk of limiting what foundations are willing to do. Surely, it confines the foundation from moving into the role of social change or convenor where results are frequently realised over the long term and cannot be measured or expressed in figures. This is further complicated by the fact that often the foundation has not been the sole actor in effecting the change, which means it cannot take sole credit.

Second, number-driven projects and programmes tied to milestones face a real danger in that the people involved lose sight of the horizon. An important perspective that frames sustainable change is actually quite simple – it takes both time and patience. Often, important challenges are not tackled because, as in the private sector, too much emphasis is placed on short-term, shareholder/stakeholder value.

Communicating the results

Strategic communications is key to a foundation's work. Externally, it is critical that results be integrated into the global communication strategy. This is more critical today than ever before, as foundations attempt to bridge the widening credibility gap between their privileged status and the perceptions of the public, including donors and stakeholders.

At KBF, the choice of whether to disseminate the results is made at the outset. However, the results of the evaluation and specific circumstances (such as current events) could influence this choice at any stage of the project or programme.

Internal communications disseminates results within the foundation at programme and management level, including the Board of Directors. External communications includes experts, key players and the specialised media and/or the general public and wider media. The local, regional, national and international dimensions are also considered.

The evaluation must also be evaluated

- Did the evaluation cycle provide what was expected?
- Were the right questions asked?
- Were good answers obtained?
- Was the right method chosen?
- Was it effective and efficient?
- Were the results properly formulated?
- Was something learned?
- Are there usable arguments for societal justification?
- Were the results provided to the right bodies and in the right way?

Evaluating the foundation

It is also important not to lose sight of the evaluation of the foundation as an entity. The adage, "the whole is more than the sum of its parts" applies in this instance. For example, to evaluate the impact or the societal appreciation of the foundation as a whole, it is not enough to simply sum up all the individual project evaluations. A more holistic method – supplementary in nature and linked to the evaluations of the components – is called for, and three aspects are central to this approach:

- The nature and size of the impact on those supported by the foundation. Here the accent lies on the assessment of increasing the capacity of the recipients.

- The nature and size of the impact on the central themes (and the relevant key actors) upon which the foundation focuses. The emphasis is on weighing the societal relevance and pertinence of the foundation's themes and of the strategic choices made.
- The nature and size of the impact on the foundation in a wider societal context; whether the foundation is viewed as an agent of change.

Particular points of interest within each of these aspects could also be included, such as gender or diversity concerns.

A counterbalance to the technocrats

As foundations grapple with the twin pressures of the accountability squeeze and the need to create value, some resort to more technocratic approaches to evaluate their work. But performance measurement has its limits and must be counterbalanced with intuitive and entrepreneurial approaches if foundations are going to succeed in overcoming their obsession with numbers and assessing their true impact on the communities they serve.

Katie Cunningham and Marc Ricks, writing in the *Stanford Social Innovation Review*,[3] state that non-profit organisations use metrics to show that they are efficient, but ask: What if donors don't care? They acknowledge that performance measurement is "one of the hottest topics in philanthropy" and present the results of a research study involving 22 individual donors that give about $50 million to charity annually. The objective of the study was to learn how these organisations wanted to see performance measurement carried out in the non-profit sector they fund.

---

[3] Katie Cunningham and Mark Ricks, "Why measure?" *Stanford Social Innovation Review*, Summer 2004, p. 44.

Only four of the 22 interviewees were strongly interested in getting better data on the performance of non-profit organisations. The rest expressed "scepticism or even outright disapproval" of the concept. The authors identified five major findings to explain this opposition:

1. Donors do not see a need for performance measurement. Metrics serve no purpose in a world that relies largely on personal connections when making decisions on grants.
2. Donors do not have time for performance measurement. They simply do not have the time or energy to scrutinise their grantees' activity.
3. Donors do not have confidence in performance measurement. The authors cite Ron Daniel, former managing partner of McKinsey & Company and the recently retired treasurer of Harvard University, who argues that metrics "have the appeal of providing measurement, but they often don't convey the essence of the phenomenon which you are trying to judge".
4. Donors do not want to see non-profit resources dedicated to perform-ance management. Many interviewees felt that measurement may be a poor use of scarce resources.
5. Donors look to institutional funders to engage in performance measure-ment on their behalf. Those who believed in the need for greater non-profit accountability noted that intermediaries already exist to conduct measurement and provide a screening mechanism for donors.

"The message from the individual donors we interviewed was loud, clear and consistent: at best, a lack of enthusiasm for performance management; at worst, outright disdain for the idea," they write.[4] At the same time, Cunningham and Ricks do not predict the death of metrics. Rather they hope their survey will inform the approach to performance measurement systems in the future.

This survey begs the question that if funders are not interested in performance management of the non-profits they fund, why should they

---

[4] Katie Cunningham and Mark Ricks, "Why measure?" *Stanford Social Innovation Review*, Summer 2004, p. 51.

be interested in applying such methodology to themselves? It also tells us that while performance measurement and metrics are important, they are not the only credible way to assess impact. They are simply tools in the toolkit of evaluation that should be used with caution.

A healthy balance must be struck between measurement and assessment if evaluation is truly to become the bedrock of accountability.

8

Philanthropy in a globalised world: Get engaged!

No matter what model of civil society foundations are working within, they are all at some point or another going to come face to face with the negative effects of globalisation as increasingly, groups of people – and in some instances, entire communities – are affected. Poverty, conflict and disease are pervasive, despite well-intentioned international declarations, targets and decrees. The twenty-first century has ushered in an era of uncertainty, with continuous marginalisation and vulnerability of populations.

This situation is exacerbated by the challenges posed by a multi-polar world, threatened by increased privatisation of hard power. The very visible manifestation of this evolution has given rise to discussions in Europe regarding the underlying complex issues concerning Islam, migration and terrorism.

It is against this backdrop that European foundations need to engage in some serious self-reflection. It is time for them to engage with other actors in civil society and attempt to map out strategies that address politically charged local, regional, national and global issues. Many foundations may view this as risky business, but it is critical. Increasingly, society expects foundations to be more than conduits for giving. They are expected to create value and they are expected to be accountable, not only at local, regional and national level, but at European and global level.

The global philanthropic community should work more on "creating alpha", says Norine MacDonald, Managing Director of the Paris-based

Gabriel Foundation and the Mercator Fund.[1] In the investment community "alpha" refers to risk-adjusted returns, that is, the difference between what is achieved by doing nothing, or maintaining the status quo (the "market return") and the actual return received. This measure is sometimes used to evaluate a manager's performance or value added. "Creating alpha" by generating results/return per unit of risk assumes that results exceed what is predicted based on the amount of risk assumed in the portfolio and that the investments are highly quantifiable in terms of risk characteristics.

"In philanthropy, our projects often have distinct risk characteristics, including political, financial and execution risks," MacDonald says. "If we apply this model to our activities, it would mean a call for increased accountability of project managers to create alpha in their projects."

In other words, to achieve results that exceed expectations, the philanthropic community, like investment managers, should be held accountable to this measure of effectiveness and impact. She adds:

> Just as in the investment community, where fund managers and their clients take a conscious decision to take on increased risk in a search for higher returns – that is, to create alpha for the investment portfolio – so must those managing philanthropic activities take on increased risk to realise an increased return from our activities.

To respond to the need for a dramatic increase in the pace of policy change, the philanthropic community must work on "creating alpha" in their project management approaches.

The accountability squeeze is escalating in the US and is likely to start echoing in the corridors of power of the European Commission and the European Parliament. Perhaps European foundations have enjoyed their unaccountable status for too long. The foundation sector has a tradition of being reactive, rather than proactive. For example, the US Council on foundations became much more successful in the

---

[1] http://www.mercatorfund.net/

1960s when faced with a threat in the form of unfavourable non-profit legislation. Europeans cannot afford to wait until the threat is at the door. It is time to be proactive.

There are already threatening rumblings from across the Atlantic, with the growing concern that US philanthropic giving could be a fund-raising front for terrorist activities at home and abroad. The US Patriot Act has brought with it a climate of uncertainty and mistrust. Numerous government measures have been introduced to address knowing or unknowing philanthropic support for terrorist activity. These rules also include the US Treasury Anti-Terrorist Financing Guidelines: *Voluntary Best Practices for US-based Charities*. Despite the "voluntary" nature of the legislation, the rules are being tightly enforced.

This climate of fear is being exported as the Bush administration is pressuring European governments to scrutinise foundations with a view to where – and to whom – their funding goes. To date, only the government of the Netherlands is trying to comply. The thin line between transparency and accountability; freedom and independence is becoming even thinner.

In the coming years, European foundations will likely be facing a changed institutional context in terms of legal and fiscal issues. Harmonisation around tax issues, particularly VAT (value added tax), could be on the horizon, as is the legal status of foundations. Today, they are operating in an environment of unfair competition arising from differences between the tax systems in the 25 member states. This could very well change.

European and American foundations together have faced huge challenges in the past – the rebuilding of Europe from the ashes of two world wars and the building and expansion of Europe into the European Union. This includes working with newly independent states and emerging market economies to strengthen civil society and build a foundation for democracy. The geopolitical context that foundations work within has been rocked by seismic shifts. As a result, today's challenges lie in countering the negative effects of globalisation, empowering communities to lift themselves out of poverty and in effecting real, sustainable societal change.

Both European and American foundations are in a privileged position to work on pressing transatlantic issues. The rift is growing wider every day as unilateral US political decisions continue to alienate Europeans and the rest of the world. Because foundations are not political actors, they can create a meaningful platform for dialogue and perhaps joint action. Reaching beyond the transatlantic dimension, they can also forge links with foundations and civil society actors – for example, in Asian and Islamic societies.

European foundations in particular need to look beyond national borders and become more European, in addition to acting on more global issues. Global problems require global solutions, but in many instances these solutions begin at home, at local level. Many European foundations are myopic, introverted and narrow in their scope. How unfortunate, when there is so much untapped potential to effect meaningful change and make a real difference.

This is not to say that funding projects at home is irrelevant. This is a plea: it is time to take what works at home, on the ground, and where feasible, ramp it up to international scale. European foundations have a duty, and a responsibility, to start building from what they know and have learned at European level to contribute to a global architecture that is more inclusive and more just. Many are doing this already. But it should become the rule, rather than the exception.

US foundations respond to global challenges

US foundations engage in international philanthropy to a greater degree than their European counterparts. US foundations and individuals, either on their own or by pooling resources, are contributing to combating large-scale problems that are left untouched by the public sector. Rien van Gendt, then executive-director of the Bernard van Leer Foundation, the Netherlands, calls this "privatisation by default".[2]

US foundations also have a "great track record" in terms of their global perspective and the international nature of their grant-making. Foundations gave an estimated $771 billion internationally in 2001, which accounted for about 15% of overall grants – an 80% increase from 1998 expenditure. This trend was probably sparked by the Bill and Melinda Gates Foundation. Partial data concerning 2002 shows that a small number of European foundations (30) give more than 5% of their annual expenditure to international programmes and projects. The overall donations are an estimated €267 million.[3]

Van Gendt points out that US foundations are responding to global challenges, including the fall of the Berlin Wall and the subsequent opening of central and eastern Europe, the end of *apartheid* in South Africa, the HIV/AIDS pandemic and environmental threats. The Bill and Melinda Gates Foundation is an obvious example. There are other examples, such as:

- The Open Society Institute has a large-scale involvement in central and eastern Europe, where it has spent hundreds of millions of dollars to create open societies.
- The Rockefeller Foundation is heavily involved in fighting HIV/AIDS in sub-Saharan African and is part of a consortium of foundations with a large budget.
- The Ford Foundation which has committed close to $300 million to an International Fellows Programme, thereby allowing 4000 graduates to study and prepare themselves as future leaders of their societies.

---

[2] Rien van Gendt, *Global Philanthropy and Future Developments*, Speech delivered at the European Foundation Leaders Summit, November 2001.

[3] The Foundation Center, "International giving more than doubled from 1998 to 2001", *New Report Shows*, October 14, 2003.

- The fall of the Berlin Wall and the collapse of *apartheid* in South Africa has stimulated the Charles Stewart Mott Foundation to commit hundreds of millions of dollars, particularly to strengthening the non-profit sector.

Van Gendt notes that US foundations are filling a void and acting as a substitute for government. When the state retreats the foundation steps in. The Rockefeller Brothers Fund report, *Global Interdependence and the Need for Social Stewardship*[4] has already remarked on the US government's retreat from international cooperative engagement, and particularly its failure to honour its commitments to multilateral agreements and organisations. The report concluded that the US has fallen behind in terms of social stewardship. This was beginning to show in 1998 under the Clinton administration, which was much admired for its multilateral approach to global affairs. Van Gendt says:

> Government insularity doesn't work any more: quite clearly global interdependence means that global trends have a large impact at the local level... it is hard to defend given the phenomenon of globalisation, which means that governments are forced to take an international perspective when addressing local problems.

As he rightly points out, there are few problems that are strictly domestic. Many connect local communities with the world at large. Consider the environment, terrorism, migration and mobility, HIV/ AIDS and climate instability. The Rockefeller Brothers Fund report defines social stewardship as:

> Efforts to promote greater social stability by fostering democracy, the rule of law, human rights, and more equitable distribution of resources. And it includes investments in human potential, such as public education and micro credit initiatives. Social stewardship is increasingly recognised as a component of national – and global – security. With the end of the Cold War, there is a growing understanding of non-military threats to peace and social stability.

---

[4] Laurie Ann Mazur and Susan E. Sechler, *Global Interdependence and the Need for Social Stewardship*, New York: Global Interdependence Initiative, The Rockefeller Brothers Fund, 1998.

Successful "social stewardship" efforts can address international problems before they metastasise into larger threats. At stake is human security.

Clearly, a greater number of US foundations have a more global agenda than their European counterparts. Van Gendt credits them with stimulating the development of civil society in central and eastern Europe – a strategic region at Europe's back door, which most European foundations have ignored. European foundations can learn from this proactive stance, but they face two challenges. The first is to look beyond their familiar national context. The second, he says, is to be more willing to take positions contrary to their national governments. Van Gendt challenges European foundations to become more open minded, more flexible and less rigid in the interpretation of their funding guidelines.

He urges European foundations to "resist transforming themselves into mainstream funders, thereby taking over the responsibilities of governments, and instead keep on doing what they do best: playing the role of innovators, incubators and catalysts".

There are European foundations that work outside national borders, but they are too often the exception. Their transnational spending often represents a very small percentage of their actual expenditure. Exceptions include, the issue-driven Bertelsmann Foundation in Germany, the Joseph Rowntree Charitable Foundation in the UK with its work in South Africa, the KBF's International Development Prize, awarded every two years, and its HIV/AIDS project in central Africa, launched in May 2003. KBFUS, a US-based charity, is, among other things, working on issues around transatlantic and international philanthropy.

The Van Leer Foundation, which focuses on helping young children, spends 95% of its grant money outside its home country. It Italy, UniCredit is modelling its fledgling foundation on its US counterparts. It spends 60% of grants on projects in Africa and has set up one of the first gift-matching programmes in Italy, matching employee donations euro for euro.

European foundations should act more European

In addition to – or even before – becoming more active global
players, European foundations should act more European. It only
makes sense in today's context – Europeans operate within a single
market using a single currency and are faced with the same challenges of globalisation. Europe's foundations need to engage outside
national borders and take on a leadership role in facing such
European challenges.

There is no shortage of pan-European challenges and issues that
must be addressed, such as: migration, education regarding the European
Community and what it means to be European, the fostering of a
European identity, racism, the R&D brain drain, how to best meet
the European Commission's target to spend 3% of its GDP on R&D,
the lack of a common foreign and security policy, the democratic deficit,
and the ageing population – to name but a few.

In short, foundations should stop their passive approach and engage.

Europe and its foundations are in a permanent paradoxical state of
mind: euro-self-denial and euro-arrogance. European foundations are
at once in awe of and irritated by the global good work of their American
counterparts. Instead of being inspired by this, the paradox has in fact
created low self-esteem. As a result, European foundations generally
keep to what they know, are afraid to take risks and continue to develop
projects within national borders.

This counterproductive attitude has created an obstacle and prevented
European foundations from reaching out to their neighbours around
the Mediterranean and beyond. There is not enough dialogue in and
around Europe on the mounting tensions we face today. When there is
contact, there is often arrogance on the Judeo-Christian European
side. And, once again, too few projects are developed to counterbalance
this. There are isolated examples of individual foundations reaching
out to create links, such as through exchange programmes of artists,
journalists, students and others, but there is no consistent, defined
strategy in this increasingly critical area.

There is a good deal of ignorance and arrogance about the Islamic world in Europe and the west, in which Islam is often judged by its more extreme manifestations. The reaction of many Islamic extremists is rooted in anger, poverty and hopelessness. Our response to this must not be simplistic, but multifaceted and long term. In the future, this will involve European foundations working together. For example, it makes no sense for a foundation to be working alone in eastern European countries. Where is the scale? However, this type of collaboration probably requires an attitude adjustment for some, as foundations are by nature individualistic and autonomous. The fact that (at the time of writing) the government of just one country – Greece – is participating in the Balkan Trust for Democracy underscores this point.

These examples make a strong case for creating a European foundation to work solely on European and global issues.

A European foundation: a wild dream?

There is currently no European foundation with a purely European geographic scope. There are foundations that tackle European issues, but these projects are marginal compared to their overall budgets. This is not the case in the US and Latin America, for example (see The AVINA Foundation, page 168).

Yet a myriad of challenges face Europe, particularly with the reintegration of the European Union from 15 to 25 members. The European Foundation Centre's (EFC) *Europe in the World* advocacy campaign was launched by the International Committee to mobilise leadership. One of the EFC's objectives is to persuade an ever-growing group of funders to increase, by 1% each year for the next five years, the expenditure they devote to initiatives outside Europe or within Europe, but with a global dimension.

It is hoped that this branding will galvanise the sector to share knowledge both within the foundation world and with its partners, with a view towards working together to tackle the bigger challenge of global development issues, including poverty, health and security.

This is an important initiative, but it is just a first step. Europe needs a foundation – preferably foundations – that works on a European scale on European challenges and to take up our responsibilities on the world stage. This is not a new idea. More than 30 years ago efforts began to create a "European Foundation". An agreement was reached in 1982 on the twenty-fifth anniversary of the signing of the Treaty of Rome, but it was never ratified. The concept was to create a European foundation to be closely connected to and largely funded by the European institutions.

However, today's model would have to be different. A truly European foundation, should be backed by private funding or funding that guarantees its independence and the need for accountable agenda-setting – provided it works for public benefit. European foundations could be created by wealthy individuals or follow the networking model, which involves multiple sources of funding, including perhaps state lottery funds.

If and when these foundations will ever be created is written in the stars.

Helping to define the EU's foreign policy identity

The question of how the EU can better ensure the security of its citizens and contribute to worldwide peace and stability is becoming increasingly critical. However, foreign and security policies in Europe are still widely considered to be national responsibilities. The research and training programme, *European Foreign and Security Policy Studies*, aims to overcome this disparity through analysing and debating the feasibility of the EU's Common Foreign and Security Policy (CFSP) and the European Security and Defence Policy (ESDP).

The programme has been jointly developed by three foundations: Compagnia di San Paolo, Torino/Italy, Riksbankens Jubileumsfond, Stockholm/Sweden and VolkswagenStiftung, Hanover/Germany.

These foundations want to strengthen the European dimension in the qualification of the next generation of intellectual leaders and security experts. They believe that dominance of national approaches to international security in the academic debate and day-to-day politics should be replaced by a transnational perspective.

This initiative, launched in May 2004, gives European researchers and young professionals opportunities to conduct research at European institutions, and to build networks through workshops and other public events, thereby making an impact on the wider debate in the field of foreign and security policies. Within this thematic framework applicants can freely choose their research topics. In total, 80 to 100 researchers and young professionals are expected to participate in the research and training programme over the next four to five years.

It's in our interest

Europe's myopic view needs to change with the times. Most of the private funders in the Balkans, central and eastern Europe and the Middle East are, once again, American foundations, such as the German Marshall Fund of the United States. For example, the German Marshall Fund of the United States, the United States Agency for International Development, and the Charles Stewart Mott Foundation have joined together to create the Balkan Trust for Democracy, a unique $27 million (€21.7 million) grant-making initiative to support good governance in southeastern Europe. The Balkan Trust is the product of a public–private partnership between the organisations with opportunities for additional partners to participate. Last year the Greek government pledged €750 000 over three years to the fund.

But where are the other European foundations and the European Union? They are busy wringing their hands over the fact that their American colleagues are exporting typically American legal and political models. European foundations should be actively engaged in supporting the development of civil society in these critical areas. They are in our backyard, yet we typically turn our backs on them.

European foundations find it difficult to explain to the European Commission and Parliament that they are not NGOs looking for funding, but that they can act as intermediaries. This makes them interesting partners for re-granting or other purposes. In fact, they could leverage existing European Commission initiatives by adding value with adding overhead costs. This type of efficient, effective public–private partnership, as The Balkan Trust clearly demonstrates, is a valuable example that could become a blueprint for the future.

The reintegration of Europe has made the EU the world's largest trading bloc. With this economic clout should come more political weight. As the US acts increasingly unilaterally – and there is little evidence that this will change fundamentally in the near future – the EU has an opportunity to move onto the world stage in a leadership role. European foundations should be doing exactly the same thing, in partnership with our American colleagues, when appropriate. The opportunities for action have never been greater; nor has the need.

Investing in leadership in Latin America

Swiss industrialist Stephan Schmidheiny established the AVINA Foundation in 1994 to "help the poor" in Latin America. After only a few months, he realised that there were too many poor and too little money. So he changed AVINA's mission to promote leadership for sustainable development throughout Latin America.

Schmidheiny, who also founded the World Business Council for Sustainable Development, decided to focus on leaders – the only people, he felt, who can change society. AVINA made mainly small grants. Leaders were offered partnerships for three to five years, but funding was only guaranteed for one year, with renewal being subject to meeting agreed targets.

Schmidheiny explains:

> We put leadership at the very core of our mission statement. In this way, AVINA began to define itself not as a development agency, but rather as a service organisation supporting leaders whom we found working effectively toward our shared vision. The quality and the rate of growth of our portfolio of associations with first-class leaders are proof that we have been able to make our advantage work in real life.

Later, when AVINA got involved in long-term partnerships with large organisations ranging from the Jesuits to Harvard Business School, it still saw its partners as the individual leaders. This gave AVINA the personal links with its partners which have helped it, more recently, to assist those leaders in forging local, national, and global alliances for social change.

AVINA is one of the few foundations that works with business leaders, helping them to form partnerships with social entrepreneurs. This reflects Schmidheiny's business roots and also explains the business principles and management instruments by which AVINA is run. (The very decentralised AVINA has a council of five members that meets every two months for two days; an annual meeting brings together 18 representatives from Latin America and Iberia.)

In another innovative initiative, Schmidheiny used $1.1 billion in stock to create the VIVA Trust in 2003. This trust now owns the GrupoNueva holding company, founded by Schmidheiny, which is involved in plantation forestry, construction equipment, and water systems. Its profits will fund AVINA. This simple relationship has sparked joint ventures between company and foundation – some philanthropic, some business projects motivated by social aims – throughout the region. This unique funding/ownership model is one that Schmidheiny hopes other philanthropists will examine.

The work by AVINA leaders is wide-ranging, and includes: supporting a micro lending programme in Argentina's remote Puna region; a programme to help sick and poor children in Rio de Janeiro that also focuses on vocational training for the parents; supporting industrial reform in the Gulf of Mexico region; creating links that strengthen the relationship between civil society and business in Brazil; funding an advocacy organisation that supports women's rights; helping soybean farmers to become more sustainable and thus preserving wetlands; creating a network of Latin American business schools; and supporting a farmers' cooperative in Paraguay.

What all of these projects have in common is that they are considered investments in leadership for sustainable development. AVINA consciously uses the term "invest" because the foundation expects these investments to generate important social and environment dividends. For this reason, partnerships are struck with leaders whose projects have tangible, meaningful effects on the areas and communities they serve.

KBF goes European

The King Baudouin Foundation officially "went European" in June 2001 when the Board reviewed its strategic plan and decided to tackle critical issues such as migration and minority rights in southeast Europe. As a result of the review, the Board changed its approach and decided to view KBF as a European foundation based in Belgium instead of a Belgian foundation located in Europe. It created a new programme line on the governance of global issues, particularly dealing with science, technology and sustainable development. European projects include a partnership with the European Policy Centre (EPC),[5] a Brussels-based think tank, to spark debate about the challenges facing the EU.

The EPC became KBF's strategic partner in 2002. Together they have organised a series of debates, EPC/KBF Migration Dialogues, about immigration in Europe. The debates are open to Belgian,

---

[5] http://www.theepc.be

European and international decision-makers and stakeholders. Because migration is tackled at local, regional, national and European level, the foundation is actively contributing to current discussions about the EU's migration policy – a highly charged pan-European issue.

Other joint initiatives include debates, conferences and studies on ethnic relations, world trade and consumer issues. Topics include *Opportunities and Challenges facing Muslim Communities: The European and the North American Experience; Beyond the Veil: Challenges and Opportunities for a Multicultural Society; Transforming the Western Balkans: A Progress Report*; and *The HIV/AIDS Pandemic: Challenges Ahead and the Role of Foundations and Civil Society*; A series of discussions took place leading up to the Cancun Trade Ministerial and the feasibility of the Doha Development Agenda, as well as several forums concerning the European consumer, food and reform of the EU's Common Agricultural Policy.

The EPC partnership enhances the foundation's image in Europe and offers a new forum to present its work.

Outside the EPC partnership, KBF initiatives deal with Islam and Muslims in Belgium and in Europe, fostering citizen participation in the European debate on the brain sciences, animal production and consumption in the twenty-first century, a trade and poverty forum, and the Transnational Giving Europe project. The latter is a network that enables donors resident in one of the participating countries to financially support non-profit organisations in other member countries while benefiting from the tax advantages provided for in the legislation of their country of residence. The KBF United States also services this purpose, adding to its mission of fostering transatlantic exchanges.

In southeast Europe, KBF supports an International Commission on the Balkans, projects for street children and youth at risk, and a living heritage initiative as well as support for the victims of trafficking in human beings. Another project is aimed at improving ethnic relations in southeast Europe.

A European statute[6]

The need for a European legal instrument is increasing in an enlarged Europe as the number of foundations that want to develop transnational cooperation, or have engaged in cross-border activity, has increased over the last decade.

A growing number of individual and other private funders have activities and assets in various EU member states. A European statute for foundations could become the appropriate legal tool for these funders to perform their work and operations across Europe.

The European Foundation Centre's EU Committee and its Legal and Tax Task Forces have produced a first proposal for the development of a European legal instrument for foundations. The EFC proposal calls for an optional European legal instrument, complementary to existing national legislations, which would be mainly governed by European law and would only apply to foundations pursuing a public benefit purpose.

The draft currently foresees that a newly created European Foundation (EF) would be registered and supervised at the European level and would have to carry out activities in at least two member states and have a minimum starting capital of €50 000.

Tax issues are controversial because the EU has limited competence in this area. The EFC proposes that an EF will be subject to the tax regime applicable to public benefit organisations in the member state in which it has its registered office. For the purpose of taxation, any gift or donation to an EF made within or across borders in the EU should be treated as if made to a public benefit organisation under the law of the member state in which the donor pays (corporate) income tax. However, for this to happen, the national legislator would have to implement appropriate tax rules.

Next steps include a lobbying campaign aimed at the European Commission, Members of the European Parliament and the member states. The EFC remains determined to push this important issue up the political agenda.

---

[6] This article is based on information from the EFC website: www.efc.be

Bridging the transatlantic divide

An emerging, important role for foundations on both sides of the Atlantic post-11 September is to work together to heal the widening rift between the United States and the rest of the world, particularly Europe. Transatlantic angst is growing, overshadowed by the US's recent proclivity towards unilateral action and its isolationist stance, coupled with its interventionist military policy. Europeans have difficulty comprehending the American state of mind because Europe is multilateral by nature. Cooperation and shared sovereignty are cornerstones of the European Union.

As a result, the American model of civil society is much different, as discussed in Chapter 2. It is an Anglo-Saxon model with a very religious complexion. Jeremy Rifkin, an American author, points out:

> Much of motivation behind American civic-mindedness can be traced back to the individualistic and religious roots of the American character. In most of Europe, by contrast, the civil society is far more secular in its orientation and less tied to the Christian notion of individual charity and more to the socialist idea of collective responsibility for the welfare of the community.[7]

The European social model is based on social cohesion: full employment, open democracy and transparency in governance are givens. In several member states, Social Democrats are a leading force and fill many of the top political posts. In America, Social Democrats are few and far between. They are usually found wielding pens, not power. In fact, the political philosophy that dominates democratic Europe is almost invisible in the United States of America.

Despite these differences, there is an ongoing dialogue between European and the more liberal American foundations. But, arguably, this is preaching to the converted. If the transatlantic divide is going to be bridged, the way forward is to open a constructive dialogue with the more conservative foundations. As Timothy E. Wirth, President of the United

---

[7] Jeremy Rifkin, *The European Dream – How Europe's Vision of the Future Is Quietly Eclipsing the American Dream*, Tarcher–Penguin, 2004, p. 34.

Nations Foundation and Better World Fund, pointed out in June 2003 (as reported in Chapter 4), the conservative US foundations have been very successful in advocating for welfare reform, school vouchers, medical savings accounts and the mainstreaming of faith-based institutions.[8]

One only has to consider the very negative ramifications of President George W. Bush's Mexico City Policy to understand how easily the current Republican/conservative US agenda can undermine the work of NGOs around the world. Also known as the Global Gag Rule, the Mexico City Policy announced in 2001 ensures that American taxpayer funds are not used to pay for reproductive health programmes in other countries. In practice, the policy continues the downward pressure on funding of reproductive health programmes world wide. Closing clinics and denying women health care can only increase the number of unwanted pregnancies in both developed and developing countries.

This action flies in the face of the Programme of Action agreed to at the International Conference on Population and Development, held in Cairo in 1994. The 179 signatories pledged to introduce and enforce national policies and programmes by 2015 that, among other things, provide access to reproductive and sexual health services, including family planning. Without the full participation of governments, many people continue to suffer from poor reproductive health, a lack of reproductive health services and choices, poverty and poor quality of life. In 2002, George W. Bush doubled the blow by withdrawing financial support to the United Nations Population Fund.

Building upon the dialogue

The transatlantic donors dialogue (TADD), launched in 1998, is intended to build bridges between European and American private

---

[8] Timothy E. Wirth, *The Need for Philanthropic Advocacy*, remarks at the Global Philanthropy Forum Conference on Borderless Giving, Stanford, California, June 2003.

and public donors who actively support and promote the development of people-to-people links and the strengthening of civil society on both sidess of the Atlantic. The TADD emerged from the Transatlantic Civil Society Dialogue, which brought together foundations, citizens' associations, government and business in a special forum to exchange information and discuss funding priorities and strategies, as well as opportunities for joint funding ventures.

The premise is good, albeit ambitious. But again, successfully addressing the fault lines in the transatlantic relationship will depend on bringing the conservative American donors into the circle. No easy task. The TADD is led by the Luso-American Development Foundation of Portugal and the German Marshall Fund of the United States with technical assistance from the Brussels-based European Foundation Centre Secretariat.

At the Transatlantic Leadership Summit held in Portugal in October 2002, Rui Machete, President of the Luso-American Development Foundation, made a plea for more concrete action:

> Not only do we need a better understanding, but we need to seek concrete answers. The gap between the US as "a state" and Europe "as states" must be diminished to improve the discussion of the most important issues such as science, innovation, global migration, terrorism, sustainable development and poverty.

Again, no easy task. There is a growing asymmetry between economic and political globalisation, to which civil society is not equipped to respond. Today's challenge is to leverage changes, find balance and influence public policy at multiple and global levels with the large institutions that play a key role in globalisation. At the same time, it is important to influence governments and public institutions towards reform and work towards distributing resources more equitably.

Europeans bring added value

Partnership with our American colleagues is essential if we are to address serious global issues. European foundations can learn valuable lessons from the American experience, both at home and internationally. Such partnerships must be based on mutual respect and in the spirit of knowledge – and cost – sharing. Rien van Gendt[9] notes that US foundations tend to take the initiative, while Europeans are less proactive and slower in their response to global challenges. In this sense, he says, "we deserve what we get".

At the same time, van Gendt points out that European foundations bring significant benefits to the partnerships they table. They have accumulated a considerable range of experiences drawn from a variety of cultures that are spread across many independent countries, each of which retains its essential national character, its own set of values, and its political structures.

He sees a missed opportunity over the past two decades for European foundations in central and eastern Europe. The problem with the American initiatives is that success in civil society in these countries is being measured against the American, Anglo-Saxon model: "How much richer this entire initiative would have been if European foundations had brought in other approaches and views, and how much better if the development of civil societies had not been constrained by having to converge on a single model," he said.

The value added of European foundations lies in the diversity they bring to relationships between the state and the private sector, the allocation and delivery of public services and they ways in which citizens are engaged in public discourse.

KBFUS – deepening transatlantic links

Established in 1997, the King Baudouin Foundation United States (KBFUS)[10] facilitates transatlantic philanthropy. KBFUS is a public

---

[9] Rien van Gendt, *Global Philanthropy and Future Developments*, Speech delivered at the European Foundation Leaders Summit, November 2001.
[10] www.kbfus.org

charity that works as a donor-advised fund and enables US-based individuals to support non-profit organisations throughout Europe in a tax-efficient way. KBFUS also works with US financial institutions, community foundations and national funds, so that together with their clients or donors, they can have a significant impact on organisations in Europe without having to navigate the complex regulations associated with international grant-making.

KBFUS also helps American corporations to create and implement effective corporate community involvement programmes in continental Europe, and assists European non-profit organisations, such as universities or cultural institutions, seeking to develop fund-raising efforts targeting US-based alumni and American visitors and friends.

In partnership with leading American foundations such as the German Marshall Fund for the United States (GMFUS) and the Charles Stewart Mott Foundation, KBFUS seeks to increase understanding between the USA and Europe. An example of this is *The Transatlantic Community Foundation Fellowship*, which was created in 2000 as a partnership with the GMFUS and with the financial support of the Charles Stewart Mott Foundation. The three-week programme enables senior staff of community foundations from the US and Europe to collaborate and exchange ideas and experiences with their colleagues across the Atlantic, and to learn about the social, cultural, and economic conditions affecting community foundations outside their own country.

Working together on global issues

International philanthropy is not a new idea. For centuries humanitarian relief efforts have turned many European and US foundations into international actors. Today, some US and European foundations are actively engaged in cross-border grant-making strategies to address poverty, political instability and disease. Yet these targeted efforts do not necessarily address the negative aspects of globalisation. Melanie Oliviero and Adele Simmons note that for some, tackling the issues of globalisation is a natural extension of their work, but for others, the topic is just too big.[11] They point out – and rightly so – that often a small amount of funding can produce significant change on a global scale. For example, the Mine Ban Treaty, the international convention to ban landmines, was promoted and achieved by a small number of civil society groups with very modest budgets.

"Whatever the scale, global challenges stemming from the integration of economies and the spread of disease across borders are increasingly moving foundations to engage directly with international trade and financial practices," they write.

The challenges societies face today are global and often require global solutions, but not always. Just because this has not been our mandate to date, or our infrastructure does not support this type of work, that does not mean we cannot do it. We should; we have an obligation to do it. Many of us are doing this already, but many more European foundations need to get engaged.

Do global challenges require a global response?

The answer to this question is: "Not necessarily." Global issues such as HIV/AIDS, the ethical challenges of the human genome, poverty, international crime, terrorism and drug policy, for example, are linked to our daily lives. This lesson was driven home in August 2004 with the kidnapping of two French journalists by the Islamic Army of Iraq, which demanded an end to the headscarf ban in state schools that came into force the first week of September. This turned a domestic "problem" into an international issue and seriously strained relations with France's five million Muslims.

---

[11] Melanie Oliviero and Adele Simmons, *The Role of Philanthropy in Globalization – intervening in the practices of the public and private sector*, p. 1.

Foundations do not necessarily need to fund initiatives outside their own countries to make a difference globally. They could help in the fight against the HIV/AIDS pandemic by pressuring national governments to live up to their international commitments for ODA (Official Development Assistance) or by contributing to the UN's Global Fund to Fight AIDS, Tuberculosis and Malaria.

Oliviero and Simmons maintain that the role of philanthropy in globalisation is not too different from its role elsewhere:

> Global problems may be large and complex, but they can be addressed at many levels, from global to local, and relatively small amounts of strategically targeted funding can lead to significant change on a large scale. Systemic change is usually the result of pressure from a number of sources, both grassroots and international.[12]

A more serious commitment to the Millennium Development Goals

In 2000 the UN developed its Millennium Development Goals (MDGs), which set targets for advancing welfare in developing countries. Annual assessments since then have been mixed. We are not on track to achieving the MDGs, despite the firm commitments of governments to do so. The aims to be achieved by 2015 are unquestionably good – to reduce extreme poverty and hunger by half; to provide universal access to primary education; to promote the equality of women; to reduce infant mortality by two-thirds; to reduce maternal mortality by three-quarters; to halt and reverse the spread of HIV/AIDS and malaria; to achieve environmental sustainability; and to form a global partnership for development.

These are goals that the international community, including the philanthropic sector, should take much more seriously.

The state of public health in the world's poorest countries is more than a human tragedy; it is an economic catastrophe. Disease-ridden

---

[12] Ibid, p. 10.

societies are much more prone to the social ills of state collapse, dislocated populations and internal violence. In addition, disease traps economies in poverty. Jeffrey Sachs' 2001 report, *Macroeconomics and Health*,[13] challenges the traditional argument that health will improve as a result of economic growth. Rather the opposite is true: improved health is critical to economic development in poor countries.

The Commission on Macroeconomics and Health report argues that for a very small fraction of rich countries' gross national product – roughly one penny for every $10 of income – it would be possible to scale up health intentions enough to save eight million lives a year, assuming that donor support is combined with realistic efforts by the poor countries themselves. In addition, the report says that by 2015–2020, increased health investments of $66 billion per year above current spending will generate at least $360 billion annually – a healthy six-fold return on investment.

In terms of health issues, there are no longer remote corners of the earth. HIV/AIDS originated in Africa in 1930 or 1940. It was not detected because of the weakness of the health systems and lack of world attention – until it surfaced in New York and San Francisco. Now the disease has spread all over the world and has affected more than 40 million people. Nearly five million people became newly infected in 2003, more than any other previous year, and three million people died. Eastern Europe and central Asia now have the world's fastest growing rates of infection. Sexually transmitted infections, including HIV/AIDS, are rising in the Newly Independent States of the former Soviet Union, particularly among young people.

HIV/AIDS targets Europe's most vulnerable: marginalized and socially excluded groups, including migrants, refugees, sex workers, men who

---

[13] *Macroeconomics and Health: Investing in health for economic development*, Report of the Commission on Macroeconomics and Health, chaired by Jeffrey D. Sachs, The World Health Organisation, December 2001.

have sex with men and injection drug users – most of whom do not have access to quality health care services.

By now we must have learned that pathogens do not carry passports, and that millions of people cross borders every day. In a disease-ridden world, this affects all of us and reinforces the fact that we live in an interconnected world where our security, physical health and economic well-being tomorrow depend on what we do today.

European HIV/AIDS Funders Group

The European HIV/AIDS Funders Group[14] is a knowledge-based network dedicated to strengthening European philanthropy in the field of HIV/AIDS. The group aims to mobilise philanthropic leadership and resources to address the global HIV/AIDS pandemic and its social and economic consequences, as well as to promote an enabling environment for independent giving.

Operated by the Network of European Foundations for Innovative Cooperation, the group's core functions include advocacy, networking and convening, coordination of peer learning and monitoring of policy and resources flows. Its objectives include:

- Fostering networking, information and best practice exchange, as well as better communication and coordination among funders active or potentially active in the field of HIV/AIDS.
- Enhancing the knowledge base and grant-making skills/capacity of donors.
- Facilitating cooperation, as well as developing new initiatives/joint ventures.
- Encouraging new donor activity.
- Interacting strategically with bilateral and multilateral institutions and supranational bodies.

---

[14] http://www.nef-web.org

Activities for 2003–2004 include mapping current strategies and grant-making of member organisations; identifying gaps and obstacles; and engaging new participants in foundations already active in the field of HIV/AIDS.

The core membership of the group comprises eight foundations and corporate European donors active or potentially active in the field. The foundation membership includes Allavida, Association François-Xavier Bagnoud, the Van Leer Foundation, Deutsche Stiftung Weltbevöklerung, Diana Princess of Wales Memorial Fund, the King Baudouin Foundation and the Nuffield Trust.

A value-added partnership for change

The Trade and Poverty Forum (TPF), a project of the German Marshall Fund of the United States, was developed in partnership with a number of foundations and other public policy institutions based in the delegation countries: The Brazilian Council on Foreign Relations; The Kind Baudouin Foundation; The Institute for Sustainable Development and International Relations (France); the Confederation of Indian Industry; the 21st Century Public Policy Institute (Japan); the Citigroup Foundation; and the Bill and Melinda Gates Foundation.

TPF brings together leaders from parliaments, businesses, labour organisations and civil society groups from leading developed and developing democracies. Its mission is to assess how the global trading system can be used to address poverty and identify a parallel agenda of public and private investments to address areas where markets fail to reach.

The focus on poverty alleviation is a core objective of the current round of World Trade Organization (WTO) negotiations launched in November 2001 at Doha, where more than 140 governments agreed to the Doha Development Agenda, which should guide their work until 2004. During the three-year Doha process, TPF is acting as a catalyst for new ideas on how trade and investment can help to serve that mission.

Previous to the WTO's September 2003 Ministerial meeting held in Cancun, Mexico, TPF published a first report of its co-chairs, *Restoring Trust in the WTO: The Challenge for Cancun*,[15] which outlined three key issues:

- Addressing poverty is both a matter of self-interest and a moral imperative.
- Trade and investment under the right conditions can be a powerful weapon in the fight against poverty.
- The WTO's development goals must not be allowed to fail. It also presented a series of preliminary recommendations, which organisations may use to inform their participation in the WTO process.

TPF's recommendations cover a broad range of issues, such as agriculture and market access, improving trade rules and building capacity, expanding access to medicines and addressing a parallel poverty agenda.

Towards an "and–and" approach

If European foundations ignore the consequences of the ongoing integration of the EU-15, and with the enlargement of the Union to 25 member states, they risk losing effectiveness. The reintegration of Europe to 25 members – and there are more to come – raises significant challenges and opportunities. At the same time, European institutions have become more important players that increasingly affect the daily lives of citizens. This dynamic presents a whole new reality for foundations that have been essentially operating within a pan-European policy vacuum. This vacuum is sure to be filled in the not-too-distant future.

---

[15] http://www.tradepovertyforum.org/

Most European foundations need to learn that, to be effective, they must work with civil society at local, regional, national and global level, assuming various roles and deploying a broad range of methodologies, depending on the context in which they operate. This is an "and–and" approach rather than a one-size fits all approach to philanthropy.

Similarly, both US and European foundations must come to terms with the daily consequences of living in a globalised, sometimes marginalised, world. For far too long, the local, national, supranational and global spheres of influence and action have been viewed as diametrically opposed.

In considering which role to play at which level – European or global – European foundations must thoroughly analyse the existing needs; determine which stakeholders are already involved, and how (through coalitions or interest groups, for example); the strength of government institutions; the political landscape; and the role played by civil society. Therein lies our strength and our value-added to society.

With the assets that foundations in the west have at their disposal, it begs the question: Do we not have an obligation, in fact a responsibility, to mobilise them to meet the enormous global challenges ahead of us?

EPILOGUE
Back to the future: The way forward

What is now proved was only once imagined.

William Blake (1757–1827)

The previous chapters have examined various ways in which foundation leaders can use a mix of methodologies and strategies to meet today's myriad of societal challenges. It is critical that those in the foundation world take the time to reflect upon the added value that often lies dormant in the sector. This added value will only be unleashed if foundation leaders and practitioners take risks by pushing the actual – and self-imposed – boundaries of the sector.

This requires a reflection back to the various roles played by the foundation, depending on the civil society in which it works and whether or not it has made a foray into the global arena. Analysing this context is critical, particularly in Europe and elsewhere, where foundations primarily operate outside the Anglo-Saxon model of civil society, where most of the American sector's activity takes place.

The US has been portrayed as a benchmark for philanthropic activity. While our colleagues on the other side of the Atlantic have done great work, it is becoming apparent that this model is not always appropriate in other societies. As argued in Chapter 1, there is a strong case for foundations to continue to fulfil the role of catalysts for social and political change, while evolving further into the role of convenor as an engaged member of civil society.

Taking value creation to a different level

No one would contend that the challenges ahead are daunting. Our globalised world is constantly changing, and at an unprecedented rate. This accelerating pace is often perceived as unmanageable, and many foundation leaders feel overwhelmed and disempowered in the face of the increasingly complex world being created by these seismic societal and global shifts, despite the significant resources of wealth – and talent – at their disposal. As they worry over how best to deploy these resources, they often end up within the narrow confines of doing what they know and hiding behind their mandate.

This book argues that foundation leaders need to think beyond their traditional scope and mobilise innovative methodologies strategically to create impact and effect meaningful change. For reasons of privilege, accountability and opportunity, we have a moral responsibility to do so. We must take value creation to a different level. Foundations – expected to be one of "the voices of civil society" – have been described by some as custodians of democracy. In fact, one could take this analogy a step further and describe them as being one of society's custodians of the future, with a mandate to create a more just world. For many, our networked global economy is exclusive and represents a threat. Opportunity for some often means social injustice and alienation for others.

But how can we chart new territory for meaningful future work? What areas should foundations be focusing on? The answers to these questions will surely differ for different societies. This final section makes a case for three avenues of work for foundations operating in western societies:

- First, they need to work towards accomplishing the tasks approved by the international community and clearly spelled out in the UN's Millennium Development Goals.
- Second, they need to focus on empowering society through democratic education and strengthening citizenship.
- The third area concerns harnessing the potential of today's technology, by striking a healthy balance between science and society.

Success in these areas will require creative, forward thinking, inspired by the known and challenged by the unknown.

Swimming towards "blue oceans"

Navigating future challenges and opportunities will not be an easy task, particularly if current trends continue. The US Council on Foundations reports that more wealth for some does not necessarily result in greater giving or philanthropic orientation. In fact, in 1990 the average American contributed about half of what he or she gave during the 1920s. "This situation, attributable to tax reforms during the Reagan era, is expected to worsen if taxes – particularly the estate tax – are lowered further, thus decreasing the financial incentive to make tax-deductible contributions."[1]

This trend may not take root in Europe or other parts of the world where the tradition of personal giving is not yet as developed as that in the US, but given the magnitude of the challenges we face, and under pressure from the accountability squeeze, human and financial resources should be deployed with great care.

To do this, foundation leaders may want to reflect upon the "blue ocean strategy", described by W. Chan Kim and Renée Mauborgne of INSEAD (France) in an October 2004 *Harvard Business Review* article. They define the business universe as consisting of two distinct kinds of space – red and blue oceans. Red oceans represent all of the industries in existence today, or the "known market space". In such oceans, industry boundaries are defined and accepted. The rules of the game are well understood. As space gets increasingly crowded, competition intensifies and the water turns bloody.

---

[1] N. Ambrose, *Philanthropy in a Time of Change – Looking forward from 2004. A Top-Level Scan of Some Anticipated Challenges as well as Opportunities for Philanthropy*, Council on Foundations, March 2004, p. 2.

Blue oceans represent all of the industries not yet in existence; the "unknown market space", untainted by competition. In blue oceans, demand is created rather than fought over. The authors write:

> There is ample opportunity for growth that is both profitable and rapid. There are two ways to create blue oceans. In a few cases, companies can give rise to completely new industries, as eBay did with the online auction industry. But in most cases, a blue ocean is created from within a red ocean when a company alters the boundaries of an existing industry.[2]

Such blue oceans are usually created from within – not beyond – red oceans of existing industries. This challenges the view that new markets are in distant waters. Rather, the authors argue, blue oceans are next to us in every industry. Their analogy of how to create value and growth that is both profitable and rapid is an invaluable perspective for foundation leaders trying to make a difference.

This book outlines at least three borders that must be challenged. The first invites a reflection upon the role of foundations. The second questions the methodology toolbox deployed by foundations and challenges practitioners to go beyond grant-making. The third presents new horizons and challenges foundations to think beyond local and national borders and gain a new geographic perspective of the world in which they live and work. Paradoxically, the book also argues that to be effective, foundation leaders must be aware of – and thoroughly understand – such borders.

Foundation leaders and practitioners at all levels need to think differently to find the "blue oceans" that certainly exist, but are waiting to be discovered, or risk drowning in a sea of mediocrity as they become increasingly incapable of fulfilling the various roles they decide to play.

---

[2] W. Chan Kim and Renée Mauborgne, "Blue ocean strategy", *Harvard Business Review*, October 2004, pp. 77–78.

Education is fundamental

The alarming upsurge of extreme right movements across Europe and the need to eliminate today's so-called "democratic deficit" has left an important space in which foundations can work. (The "democratic deficit" refers to the alientation between citizens and the European Community institutions.) As institutions that still enjoy a certain level of public trust, they can help to meet the challenges associated with these two issues and help to safeguard democracy.

The need for civic education is universal and has never been more urgent in both developed and developing societies. Foundations could also play an invaluable role in this area by forging long-term partnerships with any number of actors, inside and outside civil society. How can we expect tomorrow's citizens to deal with the democratic legacy we have handed down without educating them about the fundamental value of citizenship, which is one of the cornerstones of democracy?

Europeans have paid a heavy price for democracy. Since the end of World War II and the birth of the European Union in 1951, the notion of "social cohesion" has been at the heart of many of the EU's policies. The European Commission's cohesion policy is aimed at reducing the economic, social and territorial inequalities in standards of living and levels of opportunity. If this vision of social cohesion is to become a reality, citizens must participate in all levels of government and exercise the rights inherent in engaged citizenship.

The Council of Europe[3] recognised the importance of citizenship in proclaiming 2005 the European Year of Citizenship Through Education. The objectives include raising awareness of how education can contribute to the development of democratic citizenship and participation, which promotes social cohesion, intercultural understanding and respect for diversity and human rights. In addition, EU member states are to be provided with a framework and tools to help them

---

[3] http://www.coe.int/T/E/Cultural_Cooperation/education/E.D.C/

to reflect on the role of education in developing and promoting democratic citizenship and human rights with a view to solving concrete societal problems and favour social inclusion.

A conference organised by the German Federal Agency for Civic Education in Spain in September 2004, *Networking European Citizenship Education*, examined the need to focus on civic education outside national borders and within a European context. The agenda noted that because Europe is growing, there is need for networking the diversity in cultures and ideas and the intellectual trends of thought and discourse, making them tangible and comprehensible to citizens. Only then will a European public come into existence that is able to influence the democratic political community of the EU sustainably "bottom upwards" out of a mature European civil society.

Philanthropy can "weigh in" on behalf of civil society

In his essay *The Philanthropy/Civil Society Paradox*,[4] Bruce Sievers, executive director of the US-based Walter and Elise Haas Fund from 1983 to 2002, notes that US foundations have traditionally been taking a hands-off approach to philanthropy, which "reflects the fix-it character of American social improvement – agnostic on values but committed to improved performance". He writes: "This poses a dilemma when philanthropy seeks to address problems rooted in the disintegration of social values. The problems of civil society, reflecting weakened ethical and communal norms, pose just such a challenge to philanthropy."

Sievers argues that philanthropy has the potential to "weigh in" on behalf of civic values, but is inherently discouraged from doing so by its own structural imitations, particularly the "instrumentalism" that is a dominant theme of modern philanthropic practice. He makes a compelling case: "Among major social institutions, philanthropy has the

---

[4] Bruce Sievers, *The Philanthropy/Civil Society Paradox*, presented at the Hudson Institute's Bradley Center for Philanthropy and Civic Renewal, 17 May 2004.
http://www.hudson.org/index.cfm?fuseaction=hudson_upcoming_events&id=163

greatest capacity and freedom to direct its considerable resources toward fundamental social deficiencies of the type that weakens civil society."

Science and society: a global concern

The notion of "responsible science" is not new. However, it is becoming a growing concern as rapid advances in science, technology and innovation are bringing citizens face to face with ethical dilemmas, as well as the economic challenges to health care systems. Recent public debate concerning stem cell research is a case in point. Today, what used to be the stuff of science fiction is fast becoming our reality as scientists make quantum leaps into areas such as life sciences and biotechnology.

This holds the potential to open promising applications in health care, agricultural and food production, and environmental protection. However, debates on these issues are often restricted to scientific circles or reduced to discussions between firms and special interest groups. Citizens and civil society must be part of the process as governments develop science policy and take difficult decisions about whether or not to regulate around certain ethical questions.

The European debate on brain sciences

For example, advances in brain science over the past 10 years have raised questions about the ability of scientists to predict, modify and potentially control behaviour. This has serious implications for society. In addition, as the European population ages, the number of neuro-degenerative diseases such as Alzheimers and Parkinsons will increase substantially, leading to a huge demand for ways to alleviate or cure brain-related diseases. An important issue is how to appropriately use new treatments for neurodiseases and disorders, which are major burdens on society.

The European Citizens' Deliberation on Brain Science initiative,[5] is a two-year project involving a consortium of partners,[6] including the KBF. The project brings together 180 citizens from nine European countries to publicly evaluate and debate the topic with experts in research, policy and ethics, as well as decision-makers and other actors.

The initiative aims to create a functioning European partnership of organisations dedicated to promoting citizen involvement in the neurological sciences debate and to demonstrate the value of a citizen dialogue. In this way, the project is also contributing to the European Commission's Action Plan, *Science and Society*, launched in 2001 as a component of the European Research Area. One aspect of the Commission's strategy is to bring science policies closer to citizens.

This initiative is a clear example of how foundations can play the role of convenor, as described throughout the book, by bringing together all the stakeholders around a controversial issue. The uninformed citizen, often influenced by sensationalistic media coverage, is often fearful about the potential negative ramifications of science and technology. To survive, politicians must follow the public pulse. Corporations are looking for return on investment. Institutions, such as the European Commission, have an interest in maintaining the EU's competitiveness in this growing, important area.

Foundations are perhaps one of the few institutions that can offer a forum for debate and discussion, which hopefully will lead to more informed – and democratic – policy-making decisions.

---

[5] http://www.kbs-frb.be/code/page.cfm?id_page=125&ID=711&Cnt=EN

[6] Partners include KBF; University of Westminster, UK; Flemish Institute of Science and Technology Assessment, Belgium; Danish Board of Technology, Denmark; Cité des Sciences et de l'Industrie, France; Stiftung Deutsches Hygiene-Museum, Germany; Città della Scienza, Italy; Rathenau Institute, The Netherlands; Science Museum, UK; University of Debrecen, Hungary; Eugenides Foundation, Greece; and University of Liège, Belgium.

A call for commitment and leadership

Throughout this book, foundation leaders and practitioners are being called upon to take risks if they are to fulfil their public obligations and meet the world's future challenges. They are being asked to work locally, nationally, regionally and globally and to approach today's critical issues with an open and creative mind. They are being asked to create value and spur innovation. This is a tall order, for the contexts in which foundations operate are rife with complexities and paradoxes.

These diverse and rich environments present a huge potential. The key is in empowering giving by likewise empowering foundation leaders to have enough self-confidence to take on a leadership role in their societies. At the same time, these leaders must be aware of the political and economic forces at play. It is important to realise that we are just one of the players exercising the leverage points of change, which should, paradoxically make us more modest about what we do.

The need to be transparent and accountable has never been greater. This is one of the reasons for pursuing a strategy of active, meaningful stakeholder engagement – foundations must invest in securing their legitimacy both as privileged players and as one of the voices of civil society.

One aspect of philanthropy that should be reviewed carefully is the tendency of foundations to be caught up in the short-term, results-driven only dynamic. This can be a dangerous, downward spiral as leaders and programmers become caught up in the here-and-now rather than in creating long-term impact and value. Mark R. Kramer of the Foundation Strategy Group,[7] points out: "However good the original idea, the notion that a better approach can be invented, tested and replicated after a single trial and a few years of funding now seems improbable."

Often, true innovation and meaningful impact takes years of patient, persistent work with a view to the future rather than short-term

---

[7] Mark R. Kramer, *Redefining the Social Entrepreneur*, Perspectives for Private Foundations, Foundation Strategy Group, Spring 2004, p. 2.

returns. Kramer says that the time horizon for replication and change is "decades, not a few years" and notes that few foundations have the patience to persevere.

Leadership is essential. A strong leader knows how to invest in people as well as projects and is not afraid to take risks and fly – or fall – with the consequences. For true innovation, Kramer notes that because of natural resistance to change, the battle to get it adopted requires a person of "indomitable will, unshakeable dedication and considerable charisma". What is typically missing from the foundation model is the "unquenchable determination of a talented individual" to impose that new idea on society.

As foundations struggle to find their role in society and grapple with the daily tasks associated with programming and the accountability questions, their board members could certainly benefit by investing in and supporting strong leadership both inside and outside the foundation.

It is hoped that the book will serve as an inspiration to some, while being challenged and criticised by others, bearing in mind that foundations do not exist to be self-serving, but rather to serve our societies and communities.

Index

Index compiled by Terry Halliday